Feminist Research in Practice

Edited by

Maura Kelly
Portland State University

Barbara Gurr
University of Connecticut

ROWMAN & LITTLEFIELD
Lanham • Boulder • New York • London

Executive Editor: Rolf Janke
Editorial Assistant: Courtney Packard
Senior Marketing Manager: Amy Whitaker

Credits and acknowledgments for material borrowed from other sources, and reproduced with permission, appear on the appropriate pages within the text.

Published by Rowman & Littlefield
An imprint of The Rowman & Littlefield Publishing Group, Inc.
4501 Forbes Boulevard, Suite 200, Lanham, Maryland 20706
www.rowman.com

6 Tinworth Street, London SE11 5AL, United Kingdom

British Library Cataloguing in Publication Information Available

Library of Congress Cataloging-in-Publication Data Available

ISBN 978-1-5381-2391-1 (cloth : alk. paper)
ISBN 978-1-5381-2392-8 (pbk. : alk. paper)
ISBN 978-1-5381-2393-5 (ebook)

∞™ The paper used in this publication meets the minimum requirements of American National Standard for Information Sciences—Permanence of Paper for Printed Library Materials, ANSI/NISO Z39.48-1992.

Contents

Chapter 1

Putting Feminist Research into Practice

Maura Kelly

Sociologist Joey Sprague argues that in order to change the world, sociology, and ourselves, feminist researchers need to "ask passionately, analyze critically, and answer empoweringly" (2005, 199). Across the field of feminist sociology, and reflected in the chapters of this book, you will encounter a variety of ways in which feminist researchers engage with this challenge as we collectively contribute to scholarship on gender and inequality. Despite differences in approaches taken by feminist researchers, *understanding and challenging inequality* are at the core of feminist research. In this chapter, I give an in-depth discussion of the characteristics of feminist research.

Over time, the primary subject of feminist sociological research has shifted from a focus on *women* to *gender.* That said, some feminist scholars still emphasize that women and women's experiences should be at the core of feminist research (e.g., Bloom 1998; Devault 1999; Hesse-Biber 2014). However, in taking a broader focus on *gender*, we can explore the experiences of women, men, and non-binary people, as well as the ways in which gender works on multiple levels: individual, interactional, and institutional (Risman 2018). Feminist sociologists examine a diverse array of gendered aspects of social life, such as family, parenting, friendships, education, work, marriage and partnership, sexualities, the body, health, reproduction, religion, violence, media, politics, and activism. In each of these areas, feminist researchers aim not only to observe and explain inequality but to challenge it.

Not all research that focuses on gender and inequality is feminist. Feminist research is based on feminist methodology, that is, a feminist approach to doing research. Feminist methodology does not consist of a strict set of requirements for how feminist research ought to be conducted. Rather, feminist methodology encompasses a set of characteristics aimed at producing theo-

---

BOX 1.1
Characteristics of Feminist Research

- Acknowledges the situated knowledges we create
- Addresses the intersectional nature of inequalities and identities
- Practices reflexivity
- Produces work that is political, with implications for addressing inequality
- Contributes to conversations in critical scholarship
- Considers the role of power in the research process

---

retically informed, methodologically rigorous, ethically sound, and politically useful research. Box 1.1 summarizes the characteristics of feminist research that will be discussed in this chapter.

FEMINIST RESEARCHERS ACKNOWLEDGE THE SITUATED KNOWLEDGES WE CREATE

What kinds of knowledge can we produce with sociological research? Researchers answer that question with an epistemology, a theory about what we can know and how we can know. Mainstream sociology is dominated by positivist epistemologies, which assume that researchers can achieve scientific objectivity (knowledge is neutral and not shaped by bias, opinion, or personal experience).[1] Feminist scholars have critiqued positivist epistemologies, arguing that all research is affected by the social location of the researcher and thus produces only a partial perspective on social reality. As a result of these critiques of positivist epistemology, many feminist approaches adopt a standpoint epistemology, which has several origins, including Black feminist theory. Feminist standpoint epistemology makes the claim that knowledge production is dependent on social location and political interests (e.g., Collins 1990; Harding 1986, 2004; Smith 1990). Donna Haraway argues not for the abandonment of objectivity but for "a doctrine of embodied objectivity that accommodates paradoxical and critical feminist science projects, feminist objectivity means quite simply situated knowledges" (1988, 581). Haraway's (1988) conceptualization of situated knowledges emphasizes that all knowledge is created from a particular social location that offers a partial perspective of social reality. With this epistemological approach, feminist researchers argue that it is better to be transparent about how personal identities, experiences, and political views shape the selection of research topics as well as decisions about data collection and analysis, rather than assume these factors do not matter. For example, Barbara Gurr (chapter 13) reflects on how her own identity as a white researcher shaped her study of the water protectors at Standing Rock; she also notes how her participants' understandings of what happened at Standing Rock were shaped by their identities as Native or as white, each offering a situated knowledge from a particular social location. In sum, feminist researchers understand that any claims about social life (from the researcher or our participants) are only partial perspectives or situated knowledges.

FEMINIST RESEARCHERS ADDRESS THE INTERSECTIONAL NATURE OF INEQUALITIES AND IDENTITIES

Feminist researchers attend to intersectionality: we consider the multiple forms of inequality that affect all people (e.g., gender, race/ethnicity, class, sexuality, age, ability, nation, religion). An intersectional approach to research assesses multiple identities or systems of oppression simultaneously. Intersectionality, as developed by Black feminist scholars such as Kimberlé Crenshaw (1989, 1991) and Patricia Hill Collins (1990), has provided insights about the ways that African American women experience oppression that has both similarities to and differences from the experiences of African American men and white women. The adoption of an intersectional approach in order to avoid overgeneralizing or essentializing the experiences of a category of people has been an important contribution of feminist scholarship to mainstream sociology.

In putting intersectionality into practice in empirical research, we must confront the challenge of managing the complexity of including multiple dimensions of identity. Leslie McCall (2005) describes several approaches to intersectional research. One approach is intercategorical (research comparing across two or more intersections). For example, in the quantitative analysis of the chapter on attitudes toward science (chapter 11), my colleagues and I assess differences in attitudes toward science among white men, white women, African American men, and African American women. A second approach is intracategorical (research assessing the experiences at a single intersection). An example of this approach is the qualitative analysis of the same study in which we interviewed African American women (one unique intersection of gender and race). Regardless of the approach to intersectionality we adopt for a given project, we must manage complexity, that is, we must balance the need to assess all the dimensions of difference shaping individuals' experiences while focusing on the key identities that are most relevant for the study at hand. The goal is to be able to provide meaningful findings about differences and similarities across groups.

FEMINIST RESEARCHERS DEMONSTRATE REFLEXIVITY

Drawing on the insights of standpoint epistemology and intersectionality, feminist researchers practice reflexivity; we seek to understand how we, as researchers, influence the data collection and analysis. This includes reflecting on the researcher's positionality, that is, the researcher's identities (e.g., gender, race, class), experiences, and beliefs and how they might shape the research process. Feminist researchers do this by considering the possible consequences that might arise from the researcher's social location (particularly relative to those who are being studied) and the experience of doing research. In empirical writing, reflexivity is most often observed when feminist researchers assess how our own identities were similar and different from our participants and how these similarities (or differences) shaped data collection. For example, Joyce McNair (chapter 12) notes how her identity as an African American woman made our African American women participants more comfortable talking about racism and sexism in relation to their experiences with science. As noted above, one feminist critique of positivist research is our assertion that _all_ research is shaped by the lived experience of the researcher; thus, reflecting on how this plays out in a given study potentially results in richer, more complex, higher-quality findings.

Some feminist researchers go beyond locating themselves within the research and suggest that the emotions and experiences of the researcher may be useful in conducting research and analyzing data (Naples 2003; Sprague 2005). For example, Jo Reger (chapter 9) writes about how the twinges of emotion she experienced in her archival research led her to new paths for analysis and a deeper understanding the meaning of the work of lesbian feminist folk singer Maxine Feldman.

Manuscripts for peer-reviewed articles and book chapters in edited volumes often have a word limit that prevents feminist scholars from fully detailing their practices of reflexivity. Book-length manuscripts may provide more space for feminist scholars to be reflexive. For example, in _Reproductive Justice: The Politics of Heath Care for Native American Women_, Barbara Gurr (2015) includes an appendix on methods and methodologies. As part of this appendix, Gurr describes the role of keeping a field journal in which she wrote about interviews and observations:

> I also wrote about the emotional work of interviews for both myself and my informants; for example, how I felt when meeting a new informant (usually nervous); my personal assessment of how the informant and I attempted to establish or resist rapport with each other; and my own emotional responses to the stories shared with me during interviews are all described in these entries. (2015, 168)

In the reflective chapters in this book, we offer you opportunities to read about our contributors' reflexive processes and the ways that each project engaged with aspects of feminist methodology. The contributors' reflections on the research process and their own motivations for and location in the research do more than elucidate the myriad challenges that can arise when conducting feminist research; they also illustrate the ways such reflexivity can enrich the experience, the findings, the analysis, and even the publication of feminist work.

FEMINIST RESEARCHERS PRODUCE WORK THAT IS POLITICAL

Feminist scholars writing about feminist research have come to a consensus that feminist research must be political (Connell 2014; Hesse-Biber 2014; St. Denny 2014). With a focus on social change, feminist scholars recognize that theory alone is not sufficient. The idea of putting theory into action is sometimes referred to as praxis. For some, this means conducting research that directly benefits participants, for example, in achieving a community's political goals. For others, this means more generally promoting progressive social change. Feminist researchers do not generally attempt to specify how direct the connection must be between the research and change for the project to "count" as feminist research. However, I argue that, at a minimum, feminist research must problematize inequality and have some implications for how unequal conditions described in the research might be addressed. Of course, research intended to promote social justice is not uniquely feminist. However, it is an important characteristic of feminist research; it represents a key shared goal of feminist researchers.

Like mainstream sociological research, feminist research is often picked up by media, cited in court cases, and used to shape policy. Feminist researchers must be attentive to the way that others might apply our research after it is complete. As Katie Acosta notes (chapter 3), studying the dissolution of same-gender relationships has the potential to negatively impact queer communities; this risk has to be carefully assessed at all stages of the research process.

In the context of academic research, feminist sociological research projects are most frequently disseminated in the form of peer-reviewed journal articles, scholarly books, and scholarly edited volumes. However, given feminist researchers' commitment to social justice and promoting social change, these traditional publication avenues are generally inadequate for reaching a broader audience and creating social change. Feminist scholars (as well as sociologists working in other traditions) are experimenting with new ways to share the findings for our research. Some sociologists refer to work that is useful to broader audiences as public sociology (Burawoy 2005). Feminist scholars have noted the overlap in the goals of public sociology and the feminist commitment to social change (e.g., Acker 2005). Feminist scholars engage with public sociology in a variety of ways. For example, some feminist scholars are highly involved with social media and have significant followings, within and outside the academy. Other scholars are interviewed or write for mainstream newspapers, magazines, and online platforms to disseminate our research to broader audiences. Some feminist researchers aim to increase the policy relevance of our work by writing reports for policy makers. Others partner with community organizations, with the community organization leveraging the researchers' data to advocate for policy change or funding. Finally, some feminist scholars engaged in community research will present our research to the communities we study, for example, by speaking at meetings or events sponsored by our community partners. However, while public sociology is appealing to many feminist scholars, research in traditional publication outlets is the most highly rewarded in our discipline and there are institutional barriers and political challenges to feminist researchers who seek alternatives, such as the increased time commitment, a lack of funding opportunities, and tenure and promotion requirements (Grauerholz and Baker-Sperry 2007; Sprague and Laube 2009).

FEMINIST RESEARCHERS CONTRIBUTE TO
CONVERSATIONS IN CRITICAL SCHOLARSHIP

Like all researchers, feminist researchers are in dialogue with theory and empirical research produced by other scholars working in the same areas. Feminist researchers draw on scholarship grounded in feminist theory from sociology and related disciplines as well as critical and mainstream scholarship in sociology and related disciplines. Feminist theories and feminist research are united by the shared goal of building an understanding of gender and inequality as well as dedication to changing existing social relations. Feminist researchers use a variety of critical theories to frame our research, for example, materialist feminism, Black feminism, transnational feminism, poststructuralist feminism, queer theory, transgender theory, and critical race theory (e.g., Lorber 2012; Mann 2012). For example, Catherine Harnois (chapter 6) takes an intersectional perspective, drawing on multiracial feminism, to understand feminists' beliefs about multiple dimensions of social inequality.

Early feminist scholarship generally held an understanding of gender as binary male/female categories and rather essentialist views on the female body and womanhood. Today, feminist researchers are increasingly engaging with theoretical perspectives that reject the gender binary, understand gender as performative, and challenge essentialist ideas about gendered identities and bodies (Stryker 2007; Valocchi 2005).

Feminist research must also be in dialogue with the existing empirical research on the topic of interest. Feminist researchers explore a wide variety of issues in their scholarship. Many feminist researchers choose topics that are personally important to them; this might take the form of choosing to study people who have shared identities or experiences or choosing social problems that the researcher views as important to address to create social change.[2] For example, Katie Acosta's (chapter 3) inquiry into lesbian and queer stepparents is informed by her own experience with family. While some might view this as introducing bias into the research process, feminist researchers argue that personal connections can produce higher-quality research when intimate knowledge of the subject is paired with maintaining high standards for rigorous data collection and analysis. Feminist researchers supplement the accepted best practices of the discipline with practicing reflexivity to understand how our own identities and experiences may shape the research.

When drawing on feminist scholarship to inform a feminist methodology, feminist researchers often adopt a social constructionist perspective, emphasizing that gender categories and expectations for gendered behavior are created by society and vary across place and over time.[3] Some scholars have noted the tension between trying to maintain a social constructionist perspective and critique of the gender binary while still being able to study women (or men) as a group (Bloom 1998; McCall 2005). Leslie McCall (2005) argues for the "provisional use of categories" or acknowledging that categories are socially constructed and subject to change, but utilizing categories that have meaningful consequences for members of those categories. For example, while we understand that gender and race are socially constructed categories (i.e., systems of categorization made *meaningful* by society, not biology), we can research the ways that African American women experience exclusion from science based on their race and gender, which are meaningful categories in this context (see Kelly et al., chapter 11).

FEMINIST RESEARCHERS CONSIDER THE ROLE OF POWER IN THE RESEARCH PROCESS

Issues of power in data collection and analysis are of concern to many feminist researchers. In particular, feminist researchers call for identification of the power imbalance in the research relationship due to comparative structural locations, as well as personal characteristics, such as race/ethnicity and class (Gurr 2014; Naples 2003). Of primary concern is making sure researchers do not inappropriately exert their power over participants. However, power is not unidirectional; for example, in all research projects, potential participants have the option not to participate and the choice of what to reveal to researchers.

One feminist strategy for dealing with the power imbalance between researcher and participant is to conduct research that gives voice to marginalized people and emphasizes the perspectives of the participants. However, this is not to say that the researcher cannot provide critical analysis of these perspectives; it is the researcher who is responsible for analyzing and interpreting the data and connecting the findings to previous scholarship. For example, Emily Kane (chapter 7) reports that her participants from low-income families often adopt individual-level explanations for poverty, articulating beliefs about individual responsibility. While Kane gives voice to these participants, she also critiques the ways in which these types of individual-level explanations put undue blame on poor people; she emphasizes the importance of alternative explanations that focus on the structural conditions that lead so many people to be poor.

Another way of attending to power imbalances is to share early preliminary ideas or findings with participants (or with other members of the participants' community) to ensure that the researcher is understanding and interpreting their findings correctly; this is referred to as member checking. A final way that feminist researchers seek to address power in research is to disseminate the knowledge produced in a way appropriate to the participants or their community. Participants are often uninterested in reading journal article manuscripts or long reports; however, participants can be more engaged in alternative ways of disseminating information, such as public presentations or shorter and more accessible forms of writing.

PUTTING FEMINIST RESEARCH INTO PRACTICE

When I teach about feminist research, I outline the characteristics that I have presented here (situated knowledges, intersectionality, reflexivity, political implications, critical scholarship, and consideration of power). In the context of these discussions, students will regularly ask questions along the lines of "But aren't these just best practices for all research?" Indeed. Feminist researchers have accumulated a set of tools to produce high-quality research that serves the twin goals of understanding and challenging inequality. As I described above, the tools that feminist researchers use are shared with researchers drawing on other theoretical traditions. Some of these tools were developed by feminist researchers while others were developed elsewhere and adopted by feminist researchers.

Taking this argument a step further, I suggest that feminist research need not always have gender at the center of the analysis. While feminists argue that gender is always present, taking an intersectional perspective suggests that gender may not always be the *most* salient identity or system of inequality. For example, in Barbara Gurr's analysis of water protectors at Standing Rock (chapter 13), there are moments in which gender comes to the fore of the analysis, but on the whole, the most salient lens in this context is an analysis of indigenous and white identities.

Throughout this book, you will encounter paired chapters: an empirical chapter that describes a research study, followed by a reflective chapter in which the author(s) consider how they incorporated elements of feminist research into their study. In each set of paired chapters, you will see both a feminist approach to conducting an empirical research project and the scholars' reflection on what it means to them to do feminist research. These reflections will provide you an inside look into the research process and insight on the challenges and joys of conducting feminist research. But, more importantly, through these discussions of feminist methodology, you will see how engaging in this kind of reflexivity throughout the research process can enhance the data collection, data analysis, and writing processes.

NOTES

1. While many feminist researchers are skeptical of positivism, some adopt a positivist approach, with or without caveats about positivism.

2. This is not to discount the limitations on individuals' freedom to choose research topics, for example, expectations of faculty mentors that shape students' research agendas and concerns about funding for tenure-track faculty seeking tenure and promotion.

3. In contrast, some feminist scholarship takes up essentialist positions, emphasizing similarities among women (and among men). However, these essentialist perspectives are challenged by the need to address gender from an intersectional perspective, that is, acknowledging that we all have a variety of identities or statuses (e.g., race/ethnicity, class, gender, sexuality).

REFERENCES

Acker, Joan. 2005. "Comments on Burawoy on Public Sociology." *Critical Sociology* 31(3): 327–31.

Bloom, Leslie Rebecca. 1998. *Under the Sign of Hope: Feminist Methodology and Narrative Interpretation*. Albany: State University of New York Press.

Burawoy, Michael. 2005. "For Public Sociology." *American Sociological Review* 70(1): 4–28.

Collins, Patricia Hill. 1990. *Black Feminist Thought: Knowledge, Consciousness, and the Politics of Empowerment*. New York: Routledge.

Connell, Raewyn. 2014. "Feminist Scholarship and the Public Realm in Postcolonial Australia." *Australian Feminist Studies* 29(80): 215–30.

Crenshaw, Kimberlé. 1989. "Demarginalizing the Intersection of Race and Sex: A Black Feminist Critique of Antidiscrimination Doctrine, Feminist Theory and Antiracist Politics." *University of Chicago Legal Forum* 140(1): 139–67.

———. 1991. "Mapping the Margins: Intersectionality, Identity Politics, and Violence against Women of Color." *Stanford Law Review* 43(6): 1241–99.

Devault, Marjorie L. 1999. *Liberating Method: Feminism and Social Research*. Philadelphia: Temple University Press.

Grauerholz, Liz, and Lori Baker-Sperry. 2007. "Feminist Research in the Public Domain: Risks and Recommendations." *Gender & Society* 21(2): 272–94.

Gurr, Barbara. 2014. "Ten Years On: Making Relatives and Making Meaning in the Borderlands." *Critical Sociology* 40(1): 151–68.

———. 2015. *Reproductive Justice: The Politics of Health Care for Native American Women*. New Brunswick, NJ: Rutgers University Press.

Haraway, Donna. 1988. "Situated Knowledges: The Science Question in Feminism and the Privilege of Partial Perspective." *Feminist Studies* 14(3): 575–99.

Harding, Sandra. 1986. *The Science Question in Feminism*. Ithaca, NY: Cornell University Press.

———, ed. 2004. *The Feminist Standpoint Theory Reader: Intellectual and Political Controversies*. New York: Routledge.

Hesse-Biber, Sharlene Nagy. 2014. *Feminist Research Practice: A Primer*. Thousand Oaks, CA: Sage.

Lorber, Judith. 2012. *Gender Inequality: Feminist Theories and Politics*. New York: Oxford University Press.

Mann, Susan Archer. 2012. *Doing Feminist Theory: From Modernity to Postmodernity*. New York: Oxford University Press.

McCall, Leslie. 2005. "The Complexity of Intersectionality." *Signs: Journal of Women in Culture and Society* 30:1771–1800.

Naples, Nancy A. 2003. *Feminism and Method: Ethnography, Discourse Analysis, and Activist Research*. New York: Routledge.

Risman, Barbara. 2018. *Where the Millennials Will Take Us: A New Generation Wrestles with the Gender Structure*. New York: Oxford University Press.

Smith, Dorothy E. 1990. *The Conceptual Practices of Power: A Feminist Sociology of Knowledge*. Toronto: University of Toronto Press.

Sprague, Joey. 2005. *Feminist Methodologies for Critical Researchers: Bridging Differences*. Walnut Creek, CA: AltaMira Press.

Sprague, Joey, and Heather Laube. 2009. "Institutional Barriers to Doing Public Sociology: Experiences of Feminists in the Academy." *American Sociologist* 40(4):
249–71.

St. Denny, Emily. 2014. "'The Personal Is Political Science': Epistemological and
Methodological Issues in Feminist Social Science Research on Prostitution." *Journal of International Women's Studies* 16(1): 76–90.

Stryker, Susan. 2007. "Transgender Feminism: Queering the Woman Question." In
Third Wave Feminism, edited by Stacy Gillis, Gillian Howie, and Rebecca Mun-
ford, 59–70. New York: Palgrave Macmillan.

Valocchi, Stephen. 2005. "Not Yet Queer Enough: The Lessons of Queer Theory for
the Sociology of Gender and Sexuality." *Gender & Society* 19(6): 750–70.

Chapter 2

Overview of Sociological Research

Maura Kelly

In this chapter, I provide a brief overview of sociological research and how feminist sociologists practice it. This chapter is intended to assist you in learning the language of research design used in this book and the discipline of sociology more broadly. I begin the chapter with a discussion of the variety of research methods used by sociologists and other social scientists. I then turn to a discussion of the elements of research design you will encounter in empirical sociological research.

RESEARCH METHODS

The term *methodology* is often incorrectly used interchangeably with the term *method*. While methodology is an approach to doing research, methods are tools or techniques for collecting data. For example, in Jo Reger's analysis of feminist musician Maxine Feldman (chapter 9), she adopts a feminist *methodology* and uses the *method* of archival research. Feminist sociological research primarily utilizes the methods used in mainstream sociology; thus, there are no uniquely feminist methods. It is the questions we ask and how we answer them that make our research feminist (Harding 1986).

Some feminist researchers utilize qualitative methods, that is, methods that focus on thematic analysis and present data in the form of text, observations, or quotes. Qualitative feminist sociological researchers most commonly use content analysis, interviews, focus groups, and ethnography (see table 2.1). Some feminist sociologists also draw on alternative methods for creating knowledge, such as autoethnography. For example, in Barbara Gurr's analysis of the Native American water protectors at Standing Rock (chapter 13),

Table 2.1.   Qualitative Methods Used by Feminist Researchers

Method	Description
Qualitative content analysis, discourse analysis	A researcher codes the content of existing texts (e.g., documents, records, visual media) and presents findings using quotes and examples.
Qualitative interviews	An interviewer speaks one-on-one with participants, asking them open-ended questions about their experiences and beliefs.
Focus groups	An interviewer asks questions of participants in a group, encouraging them to talk to one another as well as to the researcher.
Ethnography, participant observation, field research	A researcher visits a field site to observe how people behave in everyday life; the researcher writes up field notes, documenting what they observe.

she incorporates autoethnography by connecting her personal experiences to broader discussions in Native scholarship.

Some feminist researchers draw on quantitative methods, that is, the statistical analysis of numeric data with results typically presented in the form of tables and figures. Quantitative analysis is usually performed using statistical software to analyze data sets. In quantitative analysis, social factors are conceptualized as variables. For example, in Catherine Harnois's study on feminist identity included in chapter 5, she uses a survey that includes variables such as *gender* (with three possible answers: male, female, and other) and *feminist* (the survey question asks, "how well does 'feminist' describe you?" with five possible answers: extremely well, very well, somewhat well, not very well, or not at all). Quantitative research can identify correlations, or relationships, between variables. To continue the previous example, Harnois finds that gender and feminist identity were correlated; specifically, women and non-binary people are more likely than men to identify with the label of feminist. Under certain conditions, the relationship between variables can be described as causation, that is, one variable causes another variable. In regression analyses with multiple variables, there are multiple predictor or dependent variables and one outcome or independent variable. Examples of quantitative methods commonly used by feminist sociologists are described in table 2.2.

Feminist research projects sometimes draw on multiple methods. Researchers using multiple methods can triangulate their findings, that is, identify consistent findings using different methods. For example, in her study of water protectors, Barbara Gurr employed ethnography, autoethnography, interviews, and content analysis. Institutional ethnography is a particular multi-method approach designed to assess interactions and power

Table 2.2. Quantitative Methods Used by Feminist Researchers

Method	Description
Quantitative content analysis	A researcher codes existing texts (e.g., documents, records, visual media) and presents statistical findings in the form of tables and figures.
Surveys	A researcher asks participants primarily closed-ended questions (via paper survey, mail, email, or phone).
Secondary analysis of survey data	A researcher analyzes survey data collected by other researchers.
Experiments	A researcher conducts a study with controlled conditions to isolate the effect of the factor being studied.

dynamics in institutions (Smith 2005). Mixed methods refers to research designs that integrate both quantitative and qualitative methods in a single study. For example, in our analysis of African American women's attitudes toward science (chapter 11), my colleagues and I first analyze quantitative survey data to identify what factors predicted attitudes toward science; we then conduct qualitative interviews to more fully understand the views held by African American women.

Researchers choose qualitative or quantitative methods to serve specific purposes. Qualitative research is best suited to understanding the complexities of populations, contexts, and processes, particularly those that are not already well known. Qualitative research is also well suited for providing descriptive and detailed data, often using the language and experiences of participants. Drawing on qualitative methods, researchers make arguments about how the social world works; these may be *causal* arguments, based on comparisons between groups, change over time, or counterfactuals (Abend, Petre, and Sauder 2013). Quantitative methods are best suited to understanding broad statistical patterns and generalizing about relationships observed in the study sample to the larger population (in research designs with random samples). Drawing on quantitative methods, researchers make arguments about the frequencies of occurrences as well as correlational and causal relationships between variables. Both qualitative and quantitative methods are useful for building and extending theory.

Mainstream quantitative sociological research often focuses on generalizability (the extension of findings from one sample to the larger population), reliability (the ability to replicate results of a study), and validity (the ability to accurately represent reality). Some feminist researchers (and some mainstream qualitative researchers) are skeptical about these concepts as ideals for research because these concepts are based on quantitative research drawing on random samples. An alternative approach to understanding the broader applicability of research suggests that insights about social processes gained from qualitative research (and quantitative research with non-random samples) may be applied to other contexts or settings; some refer to this as transferability. For example, Katie Acosta's study of ten lesbian and queer stepparent families offers insight into the legal, social, and interpersonal experiences of these families (chapter 3). While Acosta interviews a relatively small number of individuals in one family type, her theoretical insights are broadly applicable. For example, her finding that the identity of parent is not always based on a legal or biological relationship can be applied to other family types.

RESEARCH DESIGN

Feminist sociologists most commonly adhere to established processes in our discipline for research design, that is, a systematic approach to planning and implementing data collection and analysis. Research design generally starts with a review of the scholarship, that is, a body of scholarly published writing that describes what we already know about a topic. Scholarship includes theoretical work (a theory is a proposed explanation for a social phenomenon) and empirical work (academic writing about a research project conducted by the author). After reviewing the literature, the researcher identifies a gap in our knowledge that their study will seek to fill. The researcher will then develop a research question, which articulates what the researcher wants to find out from the study. For example, Catherine Harnois's research questions are in the title of chapter 5: "Who are feminists in the United States today, and what do they believe about social inequality?" To assess these questions, she conducts a quantitative analysis of nationally representative survey data. In methods courses, students are generally told that they ought to choose the method that is best for their particular research question. In practice, however, researchers often develop a preference and expertise in either quantitative or qualitative methods and pose questions that are best answered with their method(s) of choice.

In the methods section of an empirical study, feminist researchers articulate all the elements of research design to provide context for the findings we present and to allow the reader to evaluate the strengths and weaknesses of our data collection and analysis. Careful attention should be paid to describing the method (tool for collecting data), sample (who or what is being studied), and the sampling strategy (how the researcher determined which participants or cases were to be included). In Appendix A, I provide lists of the elements of research design that should be included in methods sections for commonly used methods in sociology. All these elements represent decisions that must be made by the researcher. Feminist sociologists draw on both the standard practices of our discipline for our chosen methods and practices informed by our own approach to feminist methodology.

Quantitative researchers generally take a deductive approach to data analysis by starting with hypotheses, that is, proposed outcomes or explanations that will be tested with the data. In the data analysis process, however, quantitative researchers may identify new relationships between variables that were not included in their initial hypotheses. Quantitative researchers utilize statistical software packages to analyze data (e.g., SPSS, STATA).

Researchers' analysis of qualitative data commonly draws on both previous scholarship and themes emerging from the data, what David Thomas (2006) refers to as a general inductive approach. Once researchers have collected and organized their data (e.g., interview transcripts, ethnographic fieldnotes), they begin the data analysis process, usually referred to as coding. Coding entails systematically reviewing the data and tagging segments of text with codes (or labels) that represent reoccurring ideas across the data. Some researchers conceptualize this process as identifying the themes, that is, the most important reoccurring findings that will form the basis of the written analysis. Qualitative feminist researchers may use software (e.g., Dedoose, NVivo, Atlas.ti) to facilitate our coding processes. Many feminist researchers utilize memoing throughout the data collection and analysis process, that is, writing about potential emerging themes, asking ourselves questions, and generally reflecting on the data analysis process. Some qualitative feminist researchers draw on practices associated with grounded theory, as articulated by Barney G. Glaser and Anselm L. Strauss (2009) and Kathy Charmaz (2014), which involves cycles of coding and memoing in order to understand meaning in the data and build theories.

This book focuses on feminist research conducted in academic settings (including research by faculty, graduate student, and undergraduate student researchers). Most commonly, individual researchers or small teams of researchers conduct academic feminist research. Larger research projects can include larger research teams. A team can allow for more extensive data collection as well as opportunities to train the next generation of feminist researchers. Research teams may include sociologists and/or cross-disciplinary collaborators.

Sociologists in the academy are increasingly conducting community-based research, that is, research conducted for (and sometimes by) members of a community. One form of community-based research involves a partnership between academic researchers, who conduct the research, and a community partner organization, which may fund the project and/or facilitate data collection. For example, Emily Kane and her students partnered with a public housing authority and a local child abuse and neglect prevention agency to better understand the experiences of low-income families in their community (chapter 8). Researchers and community partners worked together to develop research questions and student researchers conducted interviews with program staff and clients. Community-based research can also take the form of program evaluation, in which researchers assess the strengths and weaknesses of a program of a partner organization. Evaluation research usually uses quantitative analysis to assess the impact or outcomes of a particular program. Evaluation researchers often also incorporate qualitative analysis in order to highlight the voices of the participants; these stories can motivate funders or stakeholders to support the program. Qualitative methods can also be useful in evaluation research when there is only a small number of individuals who have participated in the program under study.

Community-based participatory research (CBPR) is another form of community-based research in which academic researchers partner with members of a community or a community organization on research that benefits the community. Researchers may involve the community members in multiple aspects of the research project: developing the research question, collecting and analyzing data, and disseminating information back to the community.[1] CBPR projects generally take a great deal of time and funding; the researcher must have an ongoing commitment to the community and the research process, and often it is appropriate to pay community members working on the research.

FEMINIST RESEARCH IN PRACTICE

This chapter has described an overview of sociological research as it is taken up by feminist researchers. Feminist researchers combine the tools of sociological research along with the insights of feminist methodology described in chapter 1 (situated knowledges, intersectionality, reflexivity, political research, critical scholarship, and consideration of power) in order to put feminist research into practice.

NOTE

1. This type of research is also referred to as action research (AR), participatory research (PR), and participatory action research (PAR; see Lykes and Crosby 2014).

REFERENCES

Abend, Gabriel, Caitlin Petre, and Michael Sauder. 2013. "Styles of Causal Thought: An Empirical Investigation." *American Journal of Sociology* 119(3): 602–54.

Charmaz, Kathy. 2014. *Constructing Grounded Theory*. Thousand Oaks, CA: Sage.

Glaser, Barney G., and Anselm L. Strauss. 2009. *The Discovery of Grounded Theory: Strategies for Qualitative Research*. New Brunswick, NJ: Transaction.

Harding, Sandra. 1986. *The Science Question in Feminism*. Ithaca, NY: Cornell University Press.

Lykes, M. Brinton, and Alison Crosby. 2014. "Feminist Practice of Community and Participatory and Action Research." In *Feminist Research Practice: A Primer*, edited by Sharlene Hesse-Biber, 145–81. Thousand Oaks, CA: Sage.

Smith, Dorothy E. 2005. *Institutional Ethnography: A Sociology for People*. Lanham, MD: AltaMira Press.

Thomas, David. 2006. "A General Inductive Approach for Analyzing Qualitative Evaluation Data." *American Journal of Evaluation* 27: 237–46.

Chapter 3

Shared Parenting When Mommy and Momma Break Up

Katie Acosta

Recent decades have brought greater visibility to same-sex parents and with it an increase in research on these families within the social sciences (Goldberg 2013; Lewin 2004). Some of this work has focused on lesbian couples and the development of a mother identity (Hequembourg and Farrell 1999). Some work has looked at issues of legality in these homes. Many parents have not had access to second-parent adoption in their state of residence, leaving non-biological parents without legal recognition (Padavic and Butterfield 2011). Research on lesbian couples who become parents with the help of assisted reproductive technologies has explored the donor selection process (Ryan and Moras 2016). Collectively, this work offers a fairly nuanced picture of parenting in two-mom families. However, less research exists on how these families parent after a relationship dissolution. This chapter offers an empirical analysis of how shared parenting is negotiated in lesbian, bisexual, and queer stepparent families formed after a relationship dissolution. I highlight the intimacy in these families' shared parenting arrangements and note that even after parents enter new relationships some are highly successful at shared parenting among multiple parents.

Prior to *Obergefell v. Hodges* (2015), discourse around relationship dissolution for same-sex couples focused on the conundrum family law found itself in as some states waived their residency requirements for marriage licenses so that same-sex couples who did not live in a marriage equality state could access this right. Since these marriages were not recognized in these couples' state of residence, they could not access a divorce in family courts should they later need one. Some individuals who married in Massachusetts (the first US state to allow it), could have potentially waited more than ten years for a legal relationship dissolution. Much as they had done prior to *Obergefell v. Hodges*, these couples had to navigate heteronormative policies in their efforts to achieve relationship dissolution (Eeden-Moorefield et al. 2011).

In an autoethnographic account, Allen (2007) applied the concept of ambiguous loss to her mourning process after losing the family she built with her partner and their two children. The end of the relationship and losing access to her nonbiological child, Allen shares, evoked an unrecognized grief as others struggled to recognize her family as legitimate and thus could not validate her loss. Allen recalls being counseled by others to let her nonbiological child go because he wasn't "really" hers anyway. For Allen, relationship dissolution came with the loss of an opportunity to continue to parent a child she had cared for since birth.

Research on parenting after a lesbian relationship dissolution has looked at the quality of relationships between children and their biological and nonbiological parents. Goldberg and Allen (2013) explored how children with lesbian parents experienced shared parenting after their parents' relationship dissolution. They found three custody arrangements prevailed in these homes: (a) joint custody, (b) primary custody to the biological parent with regular visitation with the noncustodial parent, and (c) primary custody to the biological parent and infrequent visitation with the noncustodial parent. Respondents whose parents had joint custody reported living in very close proximity to one another. Those who reported infrequent contact with a nonbiological parent described living in different parts of the country. Most respondents did not have a legally recognized relationship with both of their parents. Interestingly, however, even in families that did obtain a second-parent adoption, respondents described their parents not utilizing the courts to determine their custody arrangements.

Goldberg and Allen's (2013) research is consistent with Gartrell and colleagues' (2011) findings on similarly formed families. In their study, half of the families had established legally recognized parent-child relationships through second-parent adoptions; the other half had not. They found that nonbiological parents who obtained a second-parent adoption were more likely to maintain contact with their children after relationship dissolution than were those without one. Further, they noted that children who were legally adopted by their nonbiological parents reported spending significantly more time with them than did those without a second-parent adoption. Still, three-quarters of the separated couples in that study were sharing custody of the children irrespective of whether they had obtained a second-parent adoption. Interestingly, the children in families with joint custody reported that the quality of the mothers' relationship was worse than did those whose nonbiological parent had less involvement in their lives. It is unclear whether this can be attributed to more tension between former partners who share custody or to tension being more visible to the children due to the nature of the shared parenting relationship.

While we are beginning to see more research on relationship dissolutions in two-mom families, we lack a nuanced understanding of the arrangements they maintain after the dissolution. The findings offered in this chapter begin to close this gap.

DATA AND METHODS

This study is based on phone interviews conducted with biological, adoptive, and/or stepparents in ten families. In eight families only one parent participated and in two families both parents (living in the same home) participated. All respondents were raising children from previous relationships and most of the children in these families had at least three active parents in their lives. Most of the study parents identified as moms or stepmoms. One family includes two moms, a stepmom, and a dad.

One advantage to conducting interviews by phone is that the study did not have to be limited geographically. Study respondents described in this chapter come from a larger study of fifty families in eighteen US states plus the District of Columbia. In the larger study, which looks at the legal, social, and interpersonal experiences of lesbian, bisexual, and queer stepparent families, I explore how the state of residence shapes respondents' legal experiences. This comparative analysis would be more difficult to accomplish with face-to-face interviews given geographic limitations. Another advantage to phone interviews is that respondents could participate in the study without having to separate themselves from their responsibilities at home. I conducted many interviews after the children had gone to bed, during naptime, or on Saturday mornings while respondents fixed breakfast for their families. Offering this flexibility made it easier for respondents without the luxury of disposable time to participate.

Interviews lasted approximately ninety minutes and were audio recorded and later transcribed. I used Nvivo to code and analyze their responses All respondents were asked to describe their parenting arrangements with the children's other parents. I used the following questions to get respondents to offer details on these relationships: What is your relationship with your children's other parents? How do you and your partner deal with holidays with the children's other parents? What do the children call you and their other parents? What kinds of relationships do the children have with extended family? These questions were strategically designed to allow respondents to share multiple facets of their relationship with their children's other parents, thus offering a more nuanced picture.

FINDINGS

The findings suggest that five of the ten families maintained strong shared parenting relationships. An additional four families maintained shared parenting arrangements that were tense but civil. One family described no parenting relationship with her child's other origin parent.

Strong Shared Parenting

Respondents who described strong shared parenting described it as a team effort. They see themselves as part of an extended parenting family. These respondents use the language of "kin" to describe their children's other parents. For instance, Emma and Zoe have two children, Rita and Riley. Emma adopted Rita while in a relationship with Abby. After they separated, Emma met Zoe and Abby became partnered with Dina. Together, Emma and Zoe expanded their family when Zoe gave birth to Riley. Zoe describes the parenting arrangement she and Emma share with Abby and Dina this way: "To me, it's almost like Abby is like a sister. You know? Even though that kind of sounds weird but they're all family." Emma and Abby remained friends after their breakup and even though both are in new relationships, Emma still goes to Abby's home whenever Rita is there just to see her daughter before heading to work in the morning. Emma notes,

> Rather than separate and say, you'll [Rita] go with this mom this Christmas and that mom that Christmas, we usually try to do it together. Again, thinking it's a better situation for Rita. And not having to make her spend it with one and not the other. Not that there hasn't been instances like where we've gone to New York, let's say, for Zoe's family and then, at that point, we do kind of do the switch back and forth, but we try not to.

Another family, Alex and Nina, also describe sharing holidays in a similar fashion. Alex and Nina are raising four-year-old Lena alongside Drea and her husband, David. Lena has two younger siblings at Drea and David's house, and will soon have a new sibling at Alex and Nina's house (Nina is currently pregnant). Like Emma's family, Alex and Nina see Drea and David as part of their extended family. When I asked Nina about the relationship she and Alex have with Drea, Nina explained, "Drea wanted to be like best friends from the get-go." Nina describes holidays this way:

If we have her [Lena] Christmas Eve then Drea gets her on Christmas Day and vice versa. So last year, Drea was going to pick her [Lena] up on Christmas morning, and she said "you know, how about we come over and maybe bring some treats? Maybe have some coffee in the morning and Lena can show me what she got at your house?" At first, I was like, "Oh God am I gonna be up for it?" but I kind of took a step back like "yeah, how special is that for Lena that she gets to show not only her momma and her daddy and her baby brother, but we all get to be there all together." So we did that again this year. When we went to pick her [Lena] up, we brought over muffins and hung out for an hour to see what she got at that house. So, it's like these little gestures do go a long way for Lena, which is nice.

For these families, strong shared parenting occurred organically as a result of an already amicable relationship dissolution and among parents who describe their connections as like kin. Still, even in these circumstances, tensions arise. For instance, Nina's family exemplifies one of the strongest shared parenting relationships in this study, but they do not describe equally sharing parenting responsibilities for Lena. Nina explains,

On one side, there is a lot of inclusion. She's [Drea] always been very welcoming to me and I'm really grateful for that because I think that there are bio moms who aren't. But I think she sort of sees herself as the main mom in the whole picture. I think that . . . like she sort of concocts the plans. She is more proactive, and I feel like Alex and I just sort of go along with the plan.

Thus, strong shared parenting patterns for the study respondents more accurately resemble three or four parents working as a team, where all parents are included but with varied degrees of involvement. The most salient characteristic of these families is that parents share the goal of not wanting their children to feel as though they have separate homes with two separate sets of parents.

One family experienced major tension during the breakup and still managed to achieve the strongest shared parenting arrangement. For them, strong shared parenting did not occur organically but is something they achieved through hard work. Natasha conceived Teddy while in a relationship with Cheryl. However, Cheryl started to have second thoughts about their relationship after Teddy's arrival. Parenting was not what she had expected and while Natasha embraced mothering wholeheartedly, Cheryl struggled. The two separated while Teddy was still a baby and began coparenting. Natasha was bitter with Cheryl for leaving her and struggled emotionally to adjust. When Marie and Natasha became romantically involved, the three began to share parenting. Natasha describes it this way:

I definitely have always been the primary parent from birth, but she [Cheryl] has consistently stayed involved. She has upheld her financial obligations, which I think is just as important for her legal child. We kept everything out of the courts in terms of custody and visitation but we do have a formal parenting agreement that was drawn up. We technically have joint custody since we are both legal parents, and so we both make decisions in terms of education and activities and health and all of that. I ultimately decide what is going to happen with him but she does stay active. We stopped overnight visits, because he was having major separation anxiety and just general anxiety with the whole situation and so with the help of a child psychologist we have been wandering through this pediatric anxiety that he is suffering from. So, I think he needed a reboot of his home, his environment, his routine, his schedule. I am pretty proud that the three of us—my wife, my ex, and myself—really worked together to make that happen. We even had her [Cheryl's] visitations at our house, so as to keep him home and to reassure him that this is his home base. I am pretty proud of that, but yeah, when my wife is cooking my ex-wife dinner, it is kind of an amazing situation.

Natasha's relationship with Cheryl is different from some of the other families introduced thus far. This family had its share of conflict early on, but they have learned to overcome those difficulties and coexist in harmony for Teddy's sake. Natasha's example of Marie cooking for Cheryl illustrates that coexistence. Sharing their living space and the intimate moments of dinner as a family is a powerful way to come together, but it is not without its awkwardness and emotional difficulties, as Marie recounts here:

Marie: I'm the one who started off this process of her [Cheryl] coming into the house. When she would come into the home initially, she would always sit right on the stairs until Teddy would indicate what he had in mind for them to do. So it would be going to the basement and watching a movie, or going outside and playing, or something. But she never came into the living room. It was awkward. She [Natasha] was angry and so Natasha was never inviting. Cheryl didn't feel invited. So I started making dinner for everyone. I hosted. Teddy needs to know that we are gonna talk about him. That we all love him. He needs to know we have some sort of relationship, because we are all adults and we can get beyond the hurt because Teddy is the one who is hurt in all this stuff.

Katie: That's really big of you.

Marie: I told her as soon as I thought about it that Cheryl should stop sitting on the stairs and start incorporating her life into the home. What she was doing was packing all the fun stuff in two hours and then leaving. Teddy just can't do that and it was just not working. Sometimes Teddy doesn't want to play with us, and that's OK. If he is doing something else, just work on your computer, just be here. Tell him you are here. You don't have to pack the fun stuff in. She started incorporating her routine into coming over and I'm still making dinner and I'm still having to do my other stuff. Then she became more comfortable with the situation. Everyone is becoming more comfortable. I'm just tired of looking at her, tired of her being in our home, tired of not having the privacy that I would like to have. I want to be with my wife and son and tired of being reminded that I'm the second. So I'm glad we are transitioning into something else because I was at a breaking point.

Katie: I completely understand how that would be difficult. Did you all ever think about just leaving?

Marie: I did once. It put everybody in a weird role. When we are all together, we are all the parents. Teddy has to respect all of us and knows that we are a parenting unit. But when Natasha and I left, it was as if Cheryl became a teenage babysitter. It just felt like she had lost the power and that put us on a higher pedestal than she was. It looked funny, and felt funny, and Teddy was getting the wrong signals. It just didn't work.

Marie's honest portrayal illustrates the sacrifices some families make to preserve strong shared parenting arrangements and the costs it incurs on their interpersonal relationships. Despite the many ups and downs that Marie and Natasha have had with Cheryl, they share the same goal of parenting as a unit rather than as separate entities.

Natasha, Marie, and Cheryl are bound to one another, not just as Teddy's parents but also in another intimate way. Natasha and Cheryl chose a donor together when trying to conceive Teddy. When Natasha became pregnant, they stored their remaining sperm vials for possible future use. After Natasha and Marie became romantically involved, they decided that they wanted to have children together. Marie wanted to have the experience of carrying a child and both wanted the new addition to be biologically related to Teddy.

Choosing a sperm donor is a very intimate decision for many couples. Families consider the donor's overall health, number of recorded births, and physical characteristics such as race/ethnicity, skin tone, and eye color. Many couples select donors whose physical characteristics match those of the non-biological parent, in order to increase the likelihood that others will legitimate them both as parents in everyday interactions (Ryan and Moras 2016). Natasha and Marie did not select a donor in this way because Natasha had already made those decisions in her previous relationship with Cheryl. It was more important for Natasha and Marie that the new baby be biologically related to Teddy than that the baby resemble both parents. Thus, they decided to use the donor that Cheryl was involved in selecting. Thus, even as Natasha and Marie look toward expanding their family together, Cheryl is part of this process.

The characteristics of strong shared parenting in this sample stand apart on account of the complex ways these families are formed. When these families become parents via assisted reproductive technologies, they make decisions about their children's biology, which carries consequences for the connections they maintain with former partners thereafter. Three study families used donor sperm vials that a previous partner had had input in selecting. While Marie and the two other stepparents who made this choice would have preferred having input in selecting their donors, this preference is set aside, creating a more intimate connection with former partners.

Surviving Shared Parenting

Respondents who were surviving shared parenting kept a greater distance from their children's other parents. Respondents described these relationships as civil but never as kin or even friends. Alice and her ex, Arlene, agreed to share custody of daughter Lexie after a long, drawn-out custody battle, several rounds of mediation, and a guardian ad litem. By then, both were in new relationships—Alice with Dana and Arlene with Peggy. Like others surviving shared parenting, Alice describes her relationship with Arlene as contentious and sometimes hostile. Lexie, whom they adopted from the foster care system, suffered from a host of very serious medical conditions. She needed a kidney transplant as a baby and suffered from complications thereafter related in part to her genetic condition but also to the neglect she experienced while living with her birth mother prior to entering foster care. Alice and Arlene's parenting agreement stipulated that, at times, Lexie's medical condition necessitated that she not be moved back and forth between their homes and that under those circumstances, Alice would visit Lexie in Arlene's home for a predetermined amount of time. After Lexie underwent bladder surgery, Alice visited her several times a week at Arlene and Peggy's home while Lexie recovered. Alice describes it this way:

> Yeah and it was very tense. One time, Lexie was like, "Mom, come upstairs. I want to show you something." They [Arlene and Peggy] called the police on me, for going upstairs. So, imagine your kid going through all this. You know? Seeing all this. So the police come and they're like "what's going on?" I'm like "My daughter, like, asked me to come upstairs and, you know, I walked upstairs."

Alice and Arlene have both integrated their new wives into parenting Lexie. But the arrangement is one where the adults aren't a team, even when parenting in the same home. They parent separately and establish clear boundaries around where and how they encounter one another. In this way, the surviving shared parenting approach is about caring for the children as separate functioning families, rather than a cohesive unit.

Madeline and Bernice are moms to seven-year-old twins Arwyn and Abby and seventeen-year-old Lianna. Bernice's former partner, Delaine, is the biological parent to all three girls. Delaine gave birth to Lianna while in a heterosexual relationship with a man who is not involved in their lives at all. The twins were conceived within Bernice and Delaine's relationship. After Bernice and Delaine's relationship dissolution, they each repartnered with other women. Bernice and Madeline began sharing parenting responsibilities with Delaine and her new partner, Nan. Arwyn and Abby have a bedroom in both homes and go back and forth between their moms every few days. Madeline has a much more flexible work schedule than Bernice does and thus does most of the pickups and dropoffs for the twins. She describes her relationship with Delaine this way:

> I think, every time I go to the house to pick them up or we have to have a face-to-face interaction, which is every other Thursday and Friday . . . I know how to be very cordial, and she is as well. I think, you know, behind closed doors it's another story, but that's OK. She and I actually had a falling out about a year ago and we sat down. We actually had to meet up at Starbucks and have a conversation and we ended up hugging it out. Just to be on the same page, because again, I understand, we are stuck together. I don't plan on going anywhere. I know that those are her kids, and we are all going to be a part of each other's lives no matter what. And so, I want us to try to work that out . . . we do separate birthday parties right now. We had a birthday party for the girls and we don't have contacts for a lot of the people at school. So when it came time to invite their friends to the birthday party, I was kinda like, OK, how do I reach out to these kids' parents, I don't really know these kids' parents, and I barely know the kids. So the girls and I made invitations, I put them in their backpacks and Bernice actually talked to both of the girls' teachers and asked if they could please help them maybe put them in the other kids' folders. They were absolutely OK with that. But there were some parents who chose not to respond and not to come. I think because we are the other parents.

Madeline and Bernice communicate with Delaine and Nan only when it is unavoidable. The girls split holidays, birthday parties, and special occasions. While all four moms are civil to one another, shared parenting is something they tolerate rather than thrive at. Still, even this family is connected to one another in particularly nuanced ways. Their teenage daughter, Lianna, only has a legal relationship to her birth mom, Delaine. As Lianna has a biological father (albeit one whom she does not know), Bernice has never had a legally recognized relationship with her. Still, after Bernice and Madeline moved in together, Lianna decided that she wanted her primary residence to be their home. Lianna does not go back and forth between her moms' homes as do Arwyn and Abby. Instead, she lives with Bernice and Madeline and visits with Delaine and Nan on an informal schedule. Whenever Lianna needs the consent of a legal parent or guardian, she must go to Delaine, but all four parents cooperate to make this possible.

Struggling to Share Parenting

One study family was unsuccessful at maintaining either of the two shared parenting arrangements described above. This family's inability to share parenting resulted in one origin parent's rights being terminated. Tammie and Danika became foster parents to Adam when he was only three months old. They knew immediately that they wanted to adopt him, and Adam's case-workers were actively searching for his forever home. Tammie and Danika began the adoption process and the following year were both named his legal parents. However, when Adam was three years old, Tammie and Danika's relationship started to deteriorate. Their problems worsened after Tammie obtained a new job several hours away and the couple decided to live in separate homes. Adam went to live with Tammie, and Danika would visit them when she had time off from work. The couple tried to work on their relationship but within a year it was clear that they had drifted apart. Tammie described their journey into coparenting as rocky at best.

> So for a long time, I tried really hard to keep the relationship between Adam and her going, because he knew her. He knew her as another mom even though she wasn't there as much, and I definitely was his primary parent. But he did know her and talked about her. So I knew that he wanted to try to keep that going and I say that because she didn't try as hard. I would bring him to her and it came to the point where I was just like scared to do it because she was living a very different kind of life. Like a much wilder sort of life. And I was like, it is not safe. She wouldn't answer when I called, so I was really worried about him. But she was still his other parent. So I was like, what am I supposed to do? Eventually, I decided that I would just stop making it happen. Like if I don't bring him to her what will she do? . . . So she just stopped and like for a whole year, didn't even see him once. And I was like what the hell is wrong with her? . . . And when I met Brooke, that was actually before Danika's rights were terminated. So she was still legally his parent for a whole other year. Eventually I was like, you know what? I'm going to let her [Brooke] adopt, because this is getting ridiculous.

Tammie and Brooke were careful not to discuss the termination of parental rights with Adam. They did, however, ask him if he was comfortable with Brooke adopting him. "We talked to Adam about it and he was, well, not about the termination, but about Brooke adopting and being his parent, since she was the one in the home and loved him and he was OK with it." Since Tammie and Danika had initially adopted Adam as a baby and since Danika had been absent from his life for so long, it is unclear how much Adam grasps that Danika was actually once his legal parent and not, for instance, simply his mom's significant other who once played an important role in his life. Nonetheless, Tammie explained that although she is unsure how much Adam understands this, she assumes that eventually as he gets older he will be able to "figure it out," because Danika's name and information is in his baby books and memory boxes from infancy. Thus, while Tammie chose not to discuss the termination with Adam, she also chose not to erase the documented history that she and Danika had created for him. While Tammie and Brooke have never as a couple shared parenting with a former partner, Adam may still one day see himself as having had more than two moms.

DISCUSSION

The families presented in this chapter display a wide range of shared parenting arrangements. Most maintained a strong or at least well-functioning shared parenting arrangement, which in many cases required a great deal of emotion work on the part of all parties involved. I attribute their resiliency in shared parenting to the intentional nature in which these families were formed. These parents prepared for these children's arrival both financially and emotionally. This, I argue, contributes to their motivation after a relationship dissolution to stay as involved as possible with their children no matter how difficult the breakup itself may have been. Further, research suggests that LGBTQ individuals build families of choice—a support network of friends and community members who sustain one another in adulthood (Weston 1991). Arguably the experience of building families of choice made these study families better equipped to share parenting after a relationship dissolution than heterosexual couples would be.

A common thread among all the study families is that legal and biological ties are not the main indicators used to navigate shared parenting. Some respondents had a legal or biological relationship with their children, others not, but respondents did not create a hierarchy based on legality or biology to organize shared parenting. Importantly, not privileging legal or biological parents did not mean that study families maintained equal parenting arrangements. Instead, many study families described one individual as responsible for coordinating the others. For Nina's family, Drea (Lena's biological mother) is the coordinator. However, Nina attributes Drea's role as coordinator of all four parents as related to her status as a stay-at-home parent, not to her status as the only biological parent. For Natasha's family, Marie (Teddy's stepparent) is the coordinator, in part because she did not have the baggage and hurt that the origin parents held toward one another after the breakup. These examples illustrate the complex factors that go into the decisions study families make regarding how to share parenting. These findings are consistent with previous research that has found that lesbian coparents socially construct their roles as parents to include two mothers and to reject cultural expectations linking motherhood to biology (Dalton and Bielby 2000). The current study adds to prior research, in suggesting that some families are successful at redefining parenthood in a way that incorporates more than two social, legal, and biological parents even after relationship dissolution. The data from this study suggest that respondents organize shared parenting based on the practical needs and resources of their individual families rather than on cultural scripts.

More research on shared parenting in lesbian, bisexual, and queer families is needed to explore the circumstances that result in their more and less successful shared parenting arrangements. Further, more research should compare shared parenting arrangements across various family forms.

REFERENCES

Allen, K. R. 2007. "Ambiguous Loss after Lesbian Couples with Children Break Up: A Case for Same-Gender Divorce." *Family Relations* 56(2): 175–83.

Dalton, S., and D. D. Bielby. 2000. "'That's Our Kind of Constellation': Lesbian Mothers Negotiate Institutionalized Understandings of Gender within the Family." *Gender & Society* 14(1): 36–61.

Eeden-Moorefield, B. V., C. R. Martell, M. Williams, and M. Preston. 2011. "Same-Sex Relationships and Dissolution: The Connection between Heteronormativity and Homonormativity." *Family Relations* 60(5): 562–71.

Gartrell, N. K., H. M. Bos, H. Peyser, A. Deck, and C. Rodas. 2011. "Family Characteristics, Custody Arrangements, and Adolescent Psychological Well-Being after Lesbian Mothers Break Up." *Family Relations* 60: 572–85.

Goldberg, A. E. 2013. "'Doing' and 'Undoing' Gender: The Meaning and Division of Housework in Same-Sex Couples." *Journal of Family Theory and Review* 5: 85–104.

Goldberg, A. E., and K. R. Allen. 2013. "Same-Sex Relationship Dissolution and LGB Stepfamily Formation: Perspectives of Young Adults with LGB Parents." *Family Relations* 62(4): 529–45.

Hequembourg, A. L., and M. P. Farrell. 1999. "Lesbian Motherhood: Negotiating Marginal-Mainstream Identities. *Gender & Society* 13: 540–57.

Lewin, E. 2004. "Does Marriage Have a Future? *Journal of Marriage and Family* 66(4): 1000–7.

Padavic, I., and J. Butterfield. 2011. "Mothers, Fathers, and 'Mathers.'" *Gender & Society* 25(2): 176–97.

Ryan, M., and A. Moras. 2016. "Race Matters in Lesbian Donor Insemination: Whiteness and Heteronormativity as Co-Constituted Narratives." *Ethnic and Racial Studies* 40(4): 579–96.

Weston, K. 1991. *Families We Choose: Lesbians, Gays, Kinship.* New York: Columbia University Press.

Chapter 4

Deep Reflexivity in Conducting Sexuality and Family Research

Katie Acosta

Emirbayer and Desmond (2011) write about the importance of scholarly deep reflexivity, which requires one to go beyond acknowledging our own social position or how that position impacts the research we produce to also reflecting on our discipline and the ways in which the academy promotes a code of silence for those of us who study racial minority groups. This code of silence magnifies racial and ethnic differences and encourages researchers to romanticize the racial minority communities they study. A similar silencing occurs for scholars doing sexualities research. For someone like myself, whose research lies at the intersections of race, sexuality, and family scholarship, the importance of engaging in deep scholarly reflexivity is compounded.

Critiques of Emirbayer and Desmond (2011) point to the practical disciplinary constraints that discourage this kind of deep reflexivity (DaCosta 2012) and favor the largely superficial reflexivity most scholars engage in. This occurs through our discipline's celebration of the pathological portraits in existing scholarship of marginalized communities. These unfavorable and one-sided portraits set up scholars like me to focus our writing on resisting these pathological views rather than developing new lines of inquiry (Moore 2011).

When I reflect upon the research I've conducted as a sociologist, I must consider: How is my research on lesbian, bisexual, and queer stepparent families impacted by my personal experiences? How does the position of LGBTQ families as the target of so much division in our current political climate influence my work? How is my research influenced by sociology's preoccupation with objectivity? This chapter reflects on these questions drawing on qualitative phone interview data with fifty women who are in same-sex stepparent households. The goal of the study is to learn about the respondents' legal, social, and interpersonal experiences doing family.

BUILDING RAPPORT OVER THE PHONE

Feminist qualitative researchers often strive to build rapport with their study respondents and to create a judgment-free environment. Achieving this goal when conducting these interviews over the phone presents its own challenges. I want to make sure that respondents do not feel as though they are talking on the phone with a stranger about such sensitive topics. To that end, in preparation for data collection, I intentionally increased my online presence by building a personal website and guest blogging on popular LGBTQ family sites. I linked my website to my academic profile so that anyone interested in learning about the lesbian, bisexual, and queer stepparent study would also learn about me as a person.

Managing my public image inherently required the support of my family. In sharing more of me as a person with potential study respondents, I also shared my spouse and our children. I used social media, social organizations, and listservs to spread the word about the study and to encourage individuals to participate. When potential respondents reached out, I responded to their inquiries with more information about the study and the informed consent documents from the institutional review board, but also with links to my personal and academic sites, my Twitter handle, and my Facebook page. This way, participants could obtain an introduction to my family and me before agreeing to share theirs.

I started every interview by explaining to participants what motivated me to conduct this research. I explained that the interview would be informal and they should feel comfortable asking any questions they had of me. I started the interview by asking each respondent, "How did you start your parenting journey?" This question encouraged participants to tell a story without making presumptions of how they became parents, to take the lead, thus allowing me to simply be a guide in the conversation. The phone interviews yielded data full of thick description. The preemptive steps I took before conducting the interviews proved fruitful in minimizing some of the potential distance between us.

THE RESEARCH IS PERSONAL

As a cisgender, queer mom to two kids whom I parent alongside my wife, conducting research on same-sex families is important to me. Since I became a mom before I met my wife, the experiences of lesbian, bisexual, and queer stepparent families were personal to me—so much so that in addition to framing my interview guide based on the trends I observe in the literature, I also allow my personal experiences to inform the focus of the interview guide.

I know both personally and professionally how much LGBTQ families are scrutinized and how easily those of us parenting in these family structures can fall into the trap of overcompensating for this stigmatization by presenting a sanitized version of ourselves for public consumption. Breaking past that sanitized public face is my first obstacle with every new family I meet for my research. I often phrase questions like this: When my wife and I got together, it was hard for our son to share our familial transition with his friends. Did your family experience anything like that? By exposing my family first, I hope to give respondents permission to share their less-than-perfect moments, without asking leading questions.

RESEARCH IS POLITICAL

In the era of Trump, conducting research on same-sex families is inherently a political act. The aftermath of marriage equality in the United States (*Obergefell v. Hodges* [2015]) has brought retaliation from conservatives seeking to protect their religious belief in the superiority of heteronormative families. These years have shown us an increase in both religious freedom bills in many US states (NCSL 2017) and bills to protect adoption agencies' right to deny services to same-sex couples (ACLU 2015). Now more than in times past, politicians are proposing and passing policies to curtail the expansion of same-sex families. These political actions serve as the backdrop before which my research on lesbian, bisexual, and queer stepparent families has taken place. It would be optimistic at best to assume that this political environment has had no bearing on the data I've collected.

As researchers, we do not have control over how our work is perceived and interpreted by others. Those of us who research marginalized populations understand all too well the culturally reductive ways in which other scholars can misappropriate our research. I straddle the desire to produce authentic knowledge with the understanding that authenticity is a double-edged sword for people (like the respondents in this study) who are members of highly scrutinized communities. In a different political climate, my main concern would be for how other academics would receive my work. In our current political climate, I struggle with the knowledge that what I write can be twisted, misconstrued, or used in ways other than as I intended by politicians interested in magnifying the instability of same-sex-parented families.

THE RESEARCH IS POLICED

The efforts I've taken to build rapport with study participants have been met with suspicion from editors and peer reviewers for the journals where I submit my work. Some reviewers have seen my efforts as potentially compromising to the validity of the data. My status as a mother parenting within a same-sex relationship has been seen as a liability; reviewers fear my personal investment in the topic could impact how I analyze the data.

Does my social position influence how research participants respond to my questions? Probably. Does that compromise the authenticity of those responses? I think not. My task then is to convince those who police the walls of the academy that my research tactics and my personal investment in my research make for good sociology. At this task, I fail just as often as I succeed. But even when I succeed, I wonder how much I've compromised in the process. How much critical reflexivity continues to go undone when I compromise? How much of my respondents' lives is silenced or oversimplified?

DISCUSSION

In the lesbian, bisexual, and queer stepparent study, I delve into the lives of families that have undergone major upheaval. These families have endured divorce, the death of a parent, financial insecurity, loss of custody of their children, and estranged parents. For the study families (or any family facing such circumstances) these transitions come with emotional and physical baggage. I find myself in a lonely intellectual space, writing about how LBQ parents and their children rebuild after a breakup. Rather than focusing on these families at their strongest place (i.e., when they work on expanding their family or as they negotiate parenting for the first time), I focus on them at their worst. My goal is to present a human and realistic depiction of these parents, complete with highs and lows. Still, I wonder if this work will contribute to the idea that same-sex-parent families are dysfunctional. I am reminded of the work of Stacey and Biblarz (2001), who noted more than a decade ago that scholars conducting research on same-sex families seemed to be favoring a "no difference" result when comparing the children raised in these families to those raised by heterosexual parents. Scholars presented a finding of no difference, Stacey and Biblarz noted, even in instances where compelling data suggested more complexity. Scholars oversimplified the observed differences between children raised in same-sex households to those raised in heterosexual households perhaps, they note, because of the political pressure. As feminist qualitative scholars, we have an obligation to unpack the pressures that we carry with us when analyzing our data. Rather than oversimplifying these complexities in the hopes of presenting our data more objectively, we could benefit from embracing the complexity that makes the work we do so rich.

I admit that there have been many times when I have allowed myself to be burdened by both disciplinary and political constraints. I have allowed these burdens to nudge me in the direction of research topics that are relatively "safe." Why have I done this? Because I feel an obligation to not expose the ugliest parts—to not contribute to the pathologizing of marginalized communities. This is because I fear those parts will be judged or misappropriated or misrepresented within a larger academy that has left us so little space within which to expand upon the plurality and complexity of our lived experiences. Reflecting on these burdens, I realize it is important for us to consider what is not written. What topics do scholars like me not consider "safe" to write about? In taking inventory of what is missing, we may gain a glimpse of how much space we have successfully carved for ourselves within the academy and how much more space is needed.

REFERENCES

ACLU. 2015. "RFRA-Style Adoption Bill Signed by Governor, ACLU of Michigan Vows Legal Challenge." https://www.aclu.org/news/rfra-style-adoption-bill-signed-governor-aclu-michigan-vows-legal-challenge.

DaCosta, Kimberly McClain. 2012. "The Tenure System, Disciplinary Boundaries, and Reflexivity." *Ethnic and Racial Studies* 35(4): 626–32.

Emirbayer, Mustafa, and Matthew Desmond. 2011. "Race and Reflexivity." *Ethnic and Racial Studies* 35(4): 574–99.

Moore, Wendy Leo. 2011. "Reflexivity, Power, and Systemic Racism." *Ethnic and Racial Studies* 35(4): 614–19.

NCSL. 2017. "2017 Religious Freedom Restoration Act Legislation." National Conference of State Legislatures. http://www.ncsl.org/research/civil-and-criminal-justice/2017-religious-freedom-restoration-act-legislation.aspx#1.

Stacey, J., and T. J. Biblarz. 2001. "(How) Does the Sexual Orientation of Parents Matter?" *American Sociological Review* 66(2): 159–83.

Chapter 5

Who Are Feminists in the United States Today, and What Do They Believe about Social Inequality?

Challenging Stereotypes with Quantitative Research

Catherine Harnois

While the stereotypes of feminists in the United States have in some ways changed over the past fifty years, the dominant image of American feminists continues to be relatively negative. Some people minimize feminism by characterizing feminists as overly privileged with no "real" cause to voice complaint. Others characterize feminist activists as selfish—interested only in their own problems and neglecting the "real" problems facing groups that are "truly" oppressed. And then of course there the more hateful stereotypes of feminists as man-haters, baby-killers, bitches, and so on.

These stereotypes, and others, are harmful in a number of ways. First, by delegitimizing feminist goals, they deter everyday people, policy makers, and social groups from working for gender equality (Bashir et al. 2013). Second, by maligning feminist activists, they discourage individuals from claiming a feminist identity (Crossley 2010; Roy, Weibust, and Miller 2007). Third, by focusing attention on feminists themselves, they individualize public discourse and draw attention away from the larger issue of gender inequality. And finally, by portraying feminists as overly privileged and narrowly self-interested, they undermine the potential for solidarity between feminists and other social justice groups.

My goal in this chapter is to examine some recently collected empirical data, to see what we might learn about who feminists are in the contemporary United States, and what they believe about gender and other forms of social inequality. Are those who claim a feminist identity more likely to be young and white, for example, than those who do not claim a feminist identity? How do the two groups differ in their beliefs about gender inequality? And what about their beliefs about other types of inequality? The data I analyze come from the 2016 American National Election Survey (ANES), which is a large-scale survey of English- and Spanish-speaking adults in the United States. Before analyzing these data, I briefly review the existing sociological research on feminist identity and feminist ideology.

BACKGROUND

Feminist scholars draw a distinction between feminist identity and feminist ideology (Harnois 2012; Schnittker, Freese, and Powell 2003). Identity refers to one's sense of self, and *feminist identity* usually refers to whether an individual describes himself or herself as a feminist. *Feminist ideology*, in contrast, encompasses the attitudes and beliefs that are generally considered part of feminism. The distinction between these two concepts is important, and is illustrated in phrases such as "I'm not a feminist, but I believe in gender equality" or "I'm not a feminist, but I know sexism is a problem that a lot of women have to deal with." Not everyone who is aware of gender inequality—not even everyone who actively fights for gender justice—self-describes as feminist, and the disconnect between feminist identity on the one hand and feminist ideology on the other might itself be related to race, class, gender, age, and other factors (Aronson 2003; Naples 1991; Reger 2012; Zucker 2004).

A number of sociological and psychological studies of the US population have investigated the factors associated with claiming a feminist *identity*. These studies suggest that women are more likely to claim a feminist identity than are men (McCabe 2005; Schnittker, Freese, and Powell 2003), and that those born between 1936 and 1955—people "whose political coming of age" coincides with the second wave of the US feminist movement, are more likely than younger or older individuals to describe themselves as feminist (Schnittker, Freese, and Powell 2003, 614). Increased educational attainment has been shown to be associated with increased likelihood of claiming a feminist identity (McCabe 2005; Peltola, Milkie, and Presser 2004), though this relationship may reflect women's experiences more strongly than men's (Schnittker, Freese, and Powell 2003). In their analysis of data from the 1992 ANES, Peltola, Milkie, and Presser (2004) found that women who described themselves as white were less likely to describe themselves as feminist compared to other racial-ethnic groups, though in their analysis of the 1996 General Social Survey (GSS) they found no racial-ethnic differences in the likelihood of individuals' claiming a feminist identity. McCabe (2005) and Schnittker, Freese, and Powell (2003), who also analyzed data from the 1996 GSS, also found that the likelihood of claiming a feminist identity did not vary across racial-ethnic groups.

Within social science research, scholars often assess feminist *ideology* by examining beliefs about gender roles (for example, whether it is ideal for men to work and for women to stay home), attitudes about abortion, and beliefs about gender inequality (e.g., Bolzendahl and Myers 2004; Schnittker, Freese, and Powell 2003). This research has found that women tend to hold more progressive gender attitudes than men; increased education is also associated with more progressive gender ideologies. Research suggests that gender ideology may differ among adults of different racial-ethnic groups in the United States, but the direction and the magnitude of these differences vary significantly according to the aspect of gender ideology considered (Harnois 2012).

The current chapter builds on the research described above in several ways. First, it analyzes data that is much more recent. The findings from the studies described above are based on data collected in the mid-1990s and are based primarily on surveys of English-speaking adults. The data I analyze here were collected two decades later (2016) and include both English- and Spanish-speaking adults in the United States.

A second contribution of the current study is that it relies upon a different way of measuring feminist identity—a measure that is more consistent with how people relate to feminism in the contemporary US context. While many previous studies (e.g., McCabe 2005; Schnittker, Freese, and Powell 2003) rely on a dichotomous variable for assessing feminism (Do you think of yourself as a feminist or not?) the analysis that follows recognizes the ambivalence and complexity that surrounds feminism and feminist identities (Aronson 2003; Crossley 2017; Reger 2012), and thus operationalizes feminist identity as more of a continuum. Rather than giving respondents two options ("Yes, feminist" or "No, not feminist"), the survey question upon which the following analyses is based asks "How well does 'feminist' describe you?" and respondents can choose any of the following: extremely well; very well; somewhat well; not very well; or not at all.

A third contribution of the current chapter is that it advances an intersectional approach for understanding and analyzing contemporary feminism. I have argued elsewhere (Harnois 2015) that, while most previous research on feminism has centralized gender, an intersectional approach urges a consideration of feminism in relation to other forms of social justice. Gender justice is inarguably a central goal of feminism, but for many people, the fight for gender justice is inseparable from the fight for other forms of equality and justice (Collins 2000; Crossley 2017; Hernández and Rehman 2002; hooks 2000). Kelly and Gauchat's (2016) more recent analysis of data from 2007–2009 supports this idea, showing that feminist identity is predictive of support for a range of social policy issues, including health care and immigration. Thus, when comparing the beliefs of self-described feminists with those who don't describe themselves as feminists, it may be useful to examine beliefs about a range of issues, rather than simply gender.

DATA AND METHODS

The main two questions in this chapter are (1) in the United States today, what are the sociodemographic characteristics associated with claiming a feminist identity? and (2) how do self-described feminists in the United States today compare with non-feminists in their beliefs about a range of social inequalities? To answer these questions, I analyze data from the 2016 ANES, which was conducted at two time points. The first round of data collection took place right before the 2016 US presidential election, in which Donald Trump ran against Hillary Clinton, and the second was a short time afterward. Respondents completed the survey in one of two ways: some had a face-to-face survey and others completed the survey online. Both forms of the survey were available in English and Spanish. The target population for the face-to-face interviews is US citizens, aged eighteen and over, living in the contiguous United States; the target population for the web survey is identical, but also includes some respondents from Hawaii and Alaska. Because responses to the survey might differ somewhat, depending on the mode of survey administration (online or face-to-face), the multivariate analyses include a variable for survey mode. More information about the survey itself is available at the ANES website.[1] The sample I analyze here includes all those respondents who provided valid answers to the survey questions analyzed below. Originally there were 4,230 respondents; due to the process of list-wise deletion, the subset I analyze is 3,285 people.

Measures

Feminist Identity is assessed with the question "How well does 'feminist' describe you?," which was asked in the preelection survey. Respondents are asked to choose one of the following options: extremely well, very well, somewhat well, not very well, or not at all. I recoded the variable on a scale of 1 to 5, where 1 corresponds to "not at all" and 5 corresponds to "extremely well."

In order to determine how those who claim a feminist identity differ from those who do not, I include a number of sociodemographic variables in the analysis. All sociodemographic characteristics come from the preelection survey. The ANES asks respondents to describe their gender, and allows three categories: male, female, and other. Of the 4,271 people who took the survey, eleven opted for "other."[2] Due to the process of list-wise deletion, two of those who selected "other" were omitted from the subsample of data analyzed here. Since only nine of the 3,285 identified with an "other" gender (less than one-half of one percent of the sample), it is difficult to make any generalizations about this group, in comparison to those who identify as male or female. Not wanting to exclude these individuals from the analysis, I group them with women. While the experiences of women and non-binary individuals are obviously not equivalent (nor are the experiences of those within either of these two gender categories), women and non-binary people are structurally disadvantaged within the contemporary gender structure (Risman 2017), and for this reason, non-binary individuals may hold views that are more similar to other women (who are also structurally disadvantaged) in comparison to men.

Respondents' racial-ethnic identity is assessed by multiple survey questions, which are detailed further in the questionnaire and methodological report on the ANES website. In the face-to-face survey, for example, respondents are asked, "Are you Spanish, Hispanic, or Latino?" This is followed with the survey question: "I am going to read you a list of five race categories. Please choose one or more races that you consider yourself to be: white; Black or African American; American Indian or Alaska Native; Asian; or Native Hawaiian or other Pacific Islander." Respondents are allowed to choose multiple categories. They are also asked, "In addition to being American, what do you consider your main ethnic group or nationality group?" The ANES dataset includes a summary variable, which combines information from all these questions into a single variable, which forms the basis of the racial-ethnic categories I use here. I analyze four racial-ethnic groups: (1) those who identify as Hispanic, Spanish, or Latino/a; (2) those who identify as Blacks and African Americans, but not Latino/a, Spanish, or Hispanic; (3) those who identify as white, but not as Latino/a, Spanish, or Hispanic; and (4) other racial ethnic groups (including those who identify with multiple racial groups). Again, my decision to group respondents in this way is not meant to assume uniformity of experience across these groups, but is rather a way to draw attention to the importance of race and ethnicity, albeit in broad strokes, for understanding and analyzing feminism.

Additional variables include those assessing educational attainment and age. In terms of education, I compare five groups: those who have not earned a high school diploma; those whose highest degree is a high school diploma; those whose highest degree is an associate's degree; a bachelor's degree; or a graduate degree. Age is likewise assessed with a series of six dummy variables for those aged 18–29, 30–39, 40–49, 50–59, 60–69, and those aged 70 and higher.

In order to determine how the beliefs of those who claim a feminist identity compare with those who do not claim a feminist identity, I include six variables (all from the postelection survey) that assess respondents' beliefs. The first questions ask about equality in broad terms: To what extent do you agree with the following statement: "Our society should do whatever is necessary to make sure that everyone has an equal opportunity to succeed." Answers ranged from strongly agree to strongly disagree, and were coded 1 to 5, with 5 indicating greater support for equal opportunity.

Five additional questions assess perceptions of relative discrimination. The ANES asks, "How much discrimination is there in the United States today against each of the following groups? A great deal, a lot, a moderate amount, a little, or none at all?" I created five different variables that assess perceptions of disadvantaged groups, relative to more privileged groups: women compared to men; transgender people compared to men; Blacks compared to whites; Hispanics compared to whites, and Muslims compared to Christians. Each of these variables ranges from −4 to 4, where a score of 4 indicates the belief that the minority group (e.g., women, Muslims) faces "a great deal of discrimination," and the privileged group (e.g., men, Christians) faces "none at all." A score of −4, in contrast, indicates that the privileged group faces "a great deal of discrimination" but the minority group faces "none at all."

After downloading the data from the ANES website, and reading through the questionnaires and *Users' Guide*, I used Stata version 13.1 to recode variables, identify cases with missing responses, and conduct the statistical analyses. The analysis proceeds in three parts. I begin with an overview of the characteristics of the subsample, presented in table 5.1. Then I conduct a series of bivariate analyses, to determine how the sociodemographic characteristics of those who describe themselves as feminist compare to those who do not. These results are shown in table 5.2. I then conduct two series of multivariate regression analyses. The first shows how various sociodemographic characteristics work together to shape the likelihood of claiming a feminist identity. The second examines how feminists and non-feminists compare on their beliefs about inequality, controlling for other characteristics.

RESULTS

Table 5.1 shows the sociodemographic characteristics of the individuals in the analysis, as well as the mean scores for the attitudinal variables analyzed here. The left-most column presents information for the total sample, and the next two columns show the characteristics of self-identified men and women/other respondents separately. The data in this table are unweighted, meaning

Table 5.1.   Unweighted Descriptive Statistics, American National Election Survey, 2016

	Total (N = 3,285)		Women and Other (N = 1,742)		Men (N = 1,543)	
	%	N	%	N	%	N
Racial-ethnic group						
Black (non-Hispanic)	9.10	299	10.68	185	7.32	114
Hispanic or Latino/a	9.80	322	8.73	151	11.02	171
White (non-Hispanic)	73.63	2419	73.54	1274	73.75	1145
Other racial-ethnic group	7.46	245	7.06	122	7.91	123
Age group						
18–29	16.41	539	15.21	264	17.76	276
30–39	18.69	614	19.69	341	17.56	273
40–49	14.64	481	15.10	262	14.13	219
50–59	18.75	616	18.54	321	18.99	295
60–69	17.26	567	16.70	289	17.89	278
70+	14.25	468	14.75	256	13.67	212
Educational attainment						
Less than high school	5.84	192	5.17	90	6.61	103
HS diploma	39.33	1292	40.13	695	38.43	598
Associate's degree	14.00	460	14.70	255	13.22	205
Bachelor's degree	23.90	785	22.39	388	25.60	397
Master's degree+	16.93	556	17.62	305	16.14	250
Survey mode (Web)	74.64	2452	75.09	1301	74.14	1151

that the means presented here describe the sample accurately, but need to be adjusted statistically before they can be used to describe the broader population of English- and Spanish-speaking US citizens aged eighteen and older. Approximately 9 percent of the sample identify as Black but non-Hispanic/Latino/a; 10 percent of the sample identify as Hispanic or Latino/a; 74 percent as white and non-Hispanic/Latino/a. These percentages are similar for men and women, but while 11 percent of women identify as Black or African American, the percentage of men in this group is smaller: 7 percent. Respondents are distributed relatively evenly across age groups; the plurality of respondents (39 percent) hold a high school diploma, but not more than that.

Table 5.2 compares the characteristics of respondents who describe themselves as feminists, compared to those individuals who do not describe themselves as feminists. For purposes of this analysis, the former group includes those who indicate that the term "feminist" describes them either somewhat well, very well, or extremely well (N = 1,187). The latter includes those who responded that the word "feminist" describes them either "not very well" or "not at all" (N = 2,098). Reading across the top row of table 5.2, we see that, of those who describe themselves as feminists, 69.38 percent describe

Table 5.2. Bivariate Comparisons (Weighted) of Self-Described Feminists and Non-Feminists, American National Election Survey, 2016

	"Feminist" describes me . . .				
	Somewhat Well, Very Well, or Extremely Well		Not Very Well, or Not at All		
	%	S.E.	%	S.E.	
Gender					
Women and other	69.38	(0.02)	41.60	(0.01)	***
Racial-ethnic group					
Black (non-Hispanic)	12.19	(0.01)	9.96	(0.01)	
Hispanic or Latino/a	12.49	(0.01)	11.53	(0.01)	
White (non-Hispanic/Latino/a)	67.04	(0.02)	71.99	(0.01)	*
Other racial-ethnic group	8.27	(0.01)	6.52	(0.01)	
Age Group					
18–29	23.05	(0.02)	20.17	(0.01)	
30–39	18.36	(0.01)	16.10	(0.01)	
40–49	14.17	(0.01)	15.86	(0.01)	
50–59	20.25	(0.01)	21.11	(0.01)	
60–69	13.36	(0.01)	15.10	(0.01)	
70+	10.79	(0.01)	11.66	(0.01)	
Educational Attainment					
Less than high school	6.55	(0.01)	9.88	(0.01)	
HS diploma	41.08	(0.02)	50.04	(0.01)	***
Associate's degree	9.94	(0.01)	13.09	(0.01)	**
Bachelor's degree	22.08	(0.01)	17.60	(0.01)	**
Master's degree+	20.35	(0.01)	9.38	(0.01)	***
	Mean	S.E.	Mean	S.E.	
Society should make sure everyone has equal opportunity	4.38	(0.03)	4.05	(0.03)	***
How much discrimination is there faced by . . .					
Women, relative to men	1.49	(0.05)	0.79	(0.03)	***
Transgender people, relative to men	2.39	(0.05)	1.64	(0.04)	***
Blacks, relative to whites	1.95	(0.05)	1.17	(0.04)	***
Hispanics, relative to whites	1.53	(0.05)	0.83	(0.03)	***
Muslims, relative to Christians	1.93	(0.05)	1.11	(0.04)	***

Note: Linearized standard errors in parentheses.
*** $p < 0.001$, ** $p < 0.01$, * $p < 0.05$

themselves as either female or "other" (not including male) in terms of their gender. Of those who do not describe themselves as feminists, 41.4 percent describe themselves as female or "other" (not including male). The asterisks to the right (***) indicate that this difference is statistically significant—

meaning that, in the general population from which the ANES sample was drawn, there is a high probability that there are gender differences in who is likely to identify as feminist. Further down, there is also an asterisk in the row corresponding to the variable, white (non-Hispanic/Latino/a). Non-Hispanic/Latino/a whites comprise approximately 67 percent of those who identify as feminists, and approximately 72 percent of those who do not describe themselves as feminists. As the single asterisk (*) corresponds to a significance level of $p < 0.05$, we can be at least 95 percent confident that, in the greater population from which the sample is drawn, non-Hispanic/Latino/a whites comprise a smaller proportion of self-identified feminists compared to those who don't describe themselves as feminists. Educational differences are also significant, with individuals holding a bachelor's or master's degree over-represented among self-described feminists. That said, of those who indicate that "feminist" describes them at least "somewhat well," almost half (41.08 + 6.55 = 47.63 percent) hold no more than a high school diploma.

In addition to showing the sociodemographic characteristics of self-described feminists and non-feminists, the bottom portion of table 5.2 shows how these groups compare in their beliefs about a range of inequalities. In contrast to those who do not claim a feminist identity, those who do report significantly higher mean scores on every aspect of inequality considered here. Feminists see higher levels of discrimination against women and trans-gender people relative to men (1.49 and 2.39 respectively compared to 0.79 and 1.64 for non-feminists). Interestingly, feminists' mean scores for relative discrimination against transgender people, Blacks, Hispanics/Latinos/as, and Muslims are as high or higher than feminists' mean scores for relative gender discrimination against women. What this suggests is that, on average, femi-nists may see racial, ethnic, and religious inequalities, as well as inequali-ties experienced by transgender people, as even more pronounced than the inequalities faced by women.

Tables 5.3 and 5.4 build on the analyses presented in table 5.2, but do so with multivariate, rather than bivariate, analyses. These models acknowledge that many factors work together to shape feminist identification and beliefs about inequality. By including multiple independent variables in the same model, we are better able to isolate the role played by each variable, control-ling for all the other variables in the model. Table 5.3 presents the results from three Ordinary Least Squares (OLS) Regression models, where the dependent variable is "How well does 'feminist' describe you?" (where 1 = not at all, and 5 = extremely well). The independent variables, those that might influ-ence the extent to which individuals describe themselves as "feminist," are presented on the left side of the table. Model 1 includes respondents of all genders; model 2 includes only women and those who identify with "other" gender (not men); and model 3 examines the predictors of feminist identities among self-identified men.

Table 5.3.   Multivariate Ordinary Least Squares Regression of Feminist Identity on Sociodemographic Characteristics, Weighted Estimates, American National Election Survey, 2016

	Model 1 (Total)	Model 2 (Women and Other Gender)	Model 3 (Men)
Gender (reference group = men)			
Women & Other	0.749***		
	(0.05)		
Racial-ethnic Group (reference group = white)			
Black (non-Hispanic)	0.103	0.181	0.028
	(0.09)	(0.12)	(0.11)
Hispanic or Latino/a	0.085	0.106	0.056
	(0.08)	(0.13)	(0.10)
Other race-ethnicity	0.10	0.0747	0.101
	(0.08)	(0.13)	(0.10)
Age Group (reference group = ages 30–39)			
18–29	0.155*	0.240*	0.077
	(0.08)	(0.12)	(0.10)
40–49	−0.127	−0.0876	−0.158
	(0.08)	(0.11)	(0.10)
50–59	−0.098	−0.045	−0.143
	(0.07)	(0.11)	(0.09)
60–69	−0.141	−0.179	−0.076
	(0.07)	(0.11)	(0.10)
70+	−0.111	−0.161	−0.044
	(0.08)	(0.11)	(0.12)
Educational Attainment (reference group = HS diploma)			
Less than high school	0.009	0.232	−0.149
	(0.10)	(0.18)	(0.10)
Associate's degree	0.006	−0.056	0.074
	(0.07)	(0.10)	(0.09)
Bachelor's degree	0.363***	0.419***	0.295***
	(0.06)	(0.09)	(0.08)
Master's degree+	0.687***	0.758***	0.588***
	(0.07)	(0.09)	(0.11)
Web-based survey (1 = yes)	−0.097	−0.14	−0.054
	(0.06)	(0.08)	(0.08)
Constant	1.641***	2.363***	1.671***
	(0.08)	(0.11)	(0.11)
Observations	3,285	1,742	1,543
R-squared	0.147	0.069	0.048

Note: Linearized standard errors in parentheses.
*** p < 0.001, ** p < 0.01, * p < 0.05

The statistically significant coefficient of gender in model 1 (0.749***) indicates that compared to men, women and those identifying with another gender score, on average, 0.749 units higher on the variable, "How well does 'feminist' describe you?" controlling for other variables in the model. This means that, when race, ethnicity, age group, and education are held constant, women and other (non-men) genders tend view "feminist" as a better descriptor of themselves than men do. Moving down the column of results for model 1, the significant coefficient next to age "18–29" shows that, compared to those respondents aged 30–39, the reference group, those aged 18–29 score 0.155 units higher on the variable for feminist identity, controlling for other factors. Education is also significant, with those holding a bachelor's degree or a graduate degree scoring significantly higher on feminist identity than those whose highest degree is a high school diploma.

Model 2 shows the results for women and "other" genders (not including men), and model 3 shows the results for men. The results are largely the same. For both groups, those with a bachelor's or graduate degree score significantly higher in terms of their feminist identity. The main difference to emerge is that, among men, age has no significant effect on feminist identity: the mean score of feminist identity among the youngest age groups (18–29) is similar to that of all other age groups, controlling for the other factors in the model.[3]

Table 5.4 shows the results from an additional set of analyses, which examine the association between strength of feminist identity and beliefs about social inequalities. In table 5.3, feminist identity was the *dependent variable*, but in table 5.4 it is the primary *independent variable* of interest: the analyses are testing whether the extent to which people embrace a feminist identity is correlated with people's beliefs about a range of social inequalities, when gender, race, ethnicity, and education are held constant.

In each of the six models considered, we see that, controlling for other variables in the model, feminist identity is associated with more progressive beliefs about social inequality. Model 1 shows that, for every unit increase on the feminist identity scale, there is a corresponding 0.13-unit increase in respondents' beliefs that "society should make sure everyone has equal opportunity," controlling for other factors in the model. In other words, the more someone thinks that the term "feminist" describes them well, the more they agree with the idea that society should ensure equal opportunity. Models 2–6 show that, even when respondents' gender, racial-ethnic identity, age, and educational attainment are held constant, stronger feminist identities are associated with increased awareness of discrimination against women, transgender people, Blacks, Hispanics, and Muslims. Other factors certainly affect beliefs

Table 5.4. Multivariate OLS Regressions of Beliefs about Inequalities, Weighted Estimates, American National Election Survey, 2016

	Model 1	Model 2	Model 3	Model 4	Model 5	Model 6
	Society should make sure everyone has equal opportunity	How much discrimination is faced by . . .				
		Women	Transgender People	Blacks	Hispanics	Muslims
Feminist Identity	0.137***	0.273***	0.310***	0.333***	0.294***	0.339***
	(0.02)	(0.03)	(0.03)	(0.03)	(0.03)	(0.03)
Gender (Reference group = men)						
Women & Other	0.05	0.200***	0.12	−0.08	−0.03	−0.07
	(0.05)	(0.06)	(0.06)	(0.06)	(0.06)	(0.07)
Racial-ethnic Group (reference group = white)						
Black (non-Hispanic)	0.331***	0.22	0.00	1.145***	0.662***	0.04
	(0.08)	(0.12)	(0.12)	(0.12)	(0.12)	(0.11)
Hispanic or Latino/a	0.195**	0.14	0.02	0.681***	0.706***	0.06
	(0.07)	(0.09)	(0.10)	(0.11)	(0.09)	(0.11)
Other race-ethnicity	0.11	−0.04	−0.09	0.250*	0.09	0.00
	(0.08)	(0.11)	(0.11)	(0.11)	(0.10)	(0.11)
Age Group (reference group = ages 30–39)						
18–29	−0.144*	0.16	−0.05	0.15	0.09	0.03
	(0.07)	(0.10)	(0.10)	(0.10)	(0.10)	(0.10)
40–49	−0.06	−0.09	−0.18	−0.14	−0.203*	−0.15
	(0.07)	(0.10)	(0.10)	(0.10)	(0.09)	(0.10)
50–59	0.04	0.00	−0.15	−0.14	−0.10	−0.11
	(0.07)	(0.09)	(0.09)	(0.09)	(0.08)	(0.09)
60–69	0.12	−0.06	−0.07	0.00	0.00	−0.03
	(0.07)	(0.09)	(0.10)	(0.09)	(0.08)	(0.10)
70+	0.10	−0.231*	−0.366***	−0.17	−0.216*	−0.329**
	(0.07)	(0.09)	(0.10)	(0.10)	(0.09)	(0.10)
Educational Attainment (reference group = HS diploma)						
Less than high school	−0.220*	−0.03	−0.06	−0.20	−0.14	−0.286*
	(0.10)	(0.12)	(0.14)	(0.13)	(0.12)	(0.14)
Associate's degree	−0.05	−0.05	0.05	0.04	−0.01	−0.05
	(0.06)	(0.07)	(0.09)	(0.08)	(0.08)	(0.10)
Bachelor's degree	−0.225***	0.11	0.163*	0.191**	0.13	0.236**
	(0.05)	(0.07)	(0.08)	(0.07)	(0.07)	(0.08)
Master's degree+	−0.08	0.301***	0.314***	0.510***	0.430***	0.428***
	(0.06)	(0.08)	(0.09)	(0.08)	(0.07)	(0.09)
Web-based Survey (1 = yes)	−0.212***	−0.02	0.12	0.12	0.158*	0.12
	(0.05)	(0.06)	(0.07)	(0.06)	(0.06)	(0.07)
Constant	4.032***	0.305**	1.150***	0.427***	0.18	0.636***
	(0.08)	(0.10)	(0.11)	(0.11)	(0.10)	(0.12)
R-squared	0.06	0.11	0.09	0.17	0.14	0.10

Note: Linearized standard errors in parentheses.
*** p < 0.001, ** p < 0.01, * p < 0.05

about inequality too. For example, respondents who identify as Black, as well as those who identify as Hispanic or Latino/a, report higher mean scores for supporting equal opportunity, and also see, on average, higher levels of relative discrimination against Blacks and Hispanics. Compared to those with a high school diploma, those with a master's degree or higher see higher relative discrimination for each social group considered. But even when education and other factors are taken into consideration, strength of feminist identity increases support for equal opportunity, and increases awareness of inequalities facing women, transgender people, Blacks, Hispanics, and Muslims. Compared to those who do not embrace a feminist identity, those who do see significantly more gender, racial-ethnic, and religious discrimination.

DISCUSSION

The main two questions I posed in this chapter were (1) in the United States today, what are the sociodemographic characteristics associated with claiming a feminist identity? and (2) how do self-described feminists differ from non-feminists in their beliefs about social inequalities? The results here suggest that there are indeed significant differences between those who do and do not consider themselves feminist, but not in the stereotypical way that dominant media representations might have us believe.

Bivariate analyses (table 5.2) showed that, compared to those who don't claim a feminist identity, those who describe themselves as feminist tend to have higher levels of education, and are less likely to identify as white (and non-Hispanic/Latino/a). Feminists also tend to see higher levels of social inequality, and, on average, also believe more strongly in the importance of equal opportunity. The multivariate analyses (table 5.3) suggest that education and gender are significant predictors of feminist identity. Compared to non-feminists, feminists tend to have higher levels of formal education. The racial-ethnic composition of feminists is similar to that of non-feminists, though the proportion of non-Hispanic whites among non-feminists may be slightly higher.

Table 5.4 shows that, even when background characteristics are taken into consideration, feminists perceive higher levels of social inequality, and, on average, believe more strongly in the importance of equal opportunity. These findings provide an important corrective to stereotypes of contemporary feminists. No evidence supports the stereotypical image of feminists as more self-interested in comparison to non-feminists. In fact, the findings suggest the opposite: the more individuals describe themselves as "feminist," the more attentive they are to inequalities of experienced by not only women, but transgender people, Blacks, Hispanics, and Muslims. These findings demonstrate empirically that feminism spans multiple inequalities and is often intersectional in nature. While in some cases those who hold a feminist identity may understand feminism as primarily about gender, the results show that, in the contemporary United States, feminist identity is linked with a consciousness of multiple social inequalities. As such, the analyses presented here underscore the importance of understanding and analyzing feminism with an intersectional framework.

NOTES

1. See https://electionstudies.org.

2. An additional forty-one respondents refused to provide an answer to this question, and these respondents are not included in this analysis. This might in part reflect a resistance strategy of gender-queer people, but we are unable to determine this with any certainty. By way of comparison, fifteen respondents refused to indicate their educational attainment, and seventy-three refused to answer the question about how well "feminist" describes them.

3. In addition to the models presented here, I conducted ordered logistic regression models. The results from the logistic models were very similar, though in the aggregated model, there is a difference between those aged 40–49 (B $= -0.285$, p $= 0.032$) and those aged 30–39. I present OLS models here for ease of interpretation.

REFERENCES

Aronson, Pamela. 2003. "Feminists or 'Postfeminists'? Young Women's Attitudes toward Feminism and Gender Relations." *Gender & Society* 17(6): 903–22.

Baca Zinn, Maxine, and Bonnie Thornton Dill. 1996. "Theorizing Difference from Multiracial Feminism." *Feminist Studies* 22(2): 321–31.

Bashir, Nadia Y., et al. 2013. "The Ironic Impact of Activists: Negative Stereotypes Reduce Social Change Influence." *European Journal of Social Psychology* 43(7): 614–26.

Bolzendahl, Catherine I., and Daniel J. Myers. 2004. "Feminist Attitudes and Support for Gender Equality: Opinion Change in Women and Men, 1974–1998." *Social Forces* 83(2): 759–89.

Collins, Patricia Hill. 2000. *Black Feminist Thought: Knowledge, Consciousness, and the Politics of Empowerment*. New York: Routledge.

Crenshaw, Kimberlé. 1989. "Demarginalizing the Intersection of Race and Sex: A Black Feminist Critique of Antidiscrimination Doctrine, Feminist Theory and Antiracist Politics." *University of Chicago Legal Forum* 139.

Crossley, Alison Dahl. 2010. "'When It Suits Me, I'm a Feminist:' International Students Negotiating Feminist Representations." *Women's Studies International Forum* 33(2).

————. 2017. *Finding Feminism: Millennial Activists and the Unfinished Gender Revolution.* New York: New York University Press.

Harnois, Catherine E. 2012. "Sociological Research on Feminism and the Women's Movement: Ideology, Identity, and Practice." *Sociology Compass* 6(10): 823–32.

————. 2015. "Race, Ethnicity, Sexuality, and Women's Political Consciousness of Gender." *Social Psychology Quarterly* 78(4): 365–86.

Hernández, Daisy, and Bushra Rehman, eds. 2002. *Colonize This!: Young Women of Color on Today's Feminism.* New York: Seal Press.

hooks, bell. 2000. *Feminist Theory: From Margin to Center.* London: Pluto Press.

Kelly, Maura, and Gordon Gauchat. 2016. "Feminist Identity, Feminist Politics: US Feminists' Attitudes toward Social Policies." *Sociological Perspectives* 59(4): 855–872.

McCabe, Janice. 2005. "What's in a Label? The Relationship between Feminist Self-identification and "Feminist" Attitudes among US Women and Men." *Gender & Society* 19(4): 480–505.

Naples, Nancy A. 1991. "'Just What Needed to Be Done': The Political Practice of Women Community Workers in Low-Income Neighborhoods." *Gender & Society* 5(4): 478–94.

Peltola, Pia, Melissa A. Milkie, and Stanley Presser. 2004. "The 'Feminist' Mystique: Feminist Identity in Three Generations of Women." *Gender & Society* 18(1): 122–44.

Reger, Jo. 2012. *Everywhere and Nowhere: Contemporary Feminism in the United States.* New York: Oxford.

Risman, Barbara J. 2017. "2016 Southern Sociological Society Presidential Address: Are Millennials Cracking the Gender Structure?" *Social Currents* 4(3): 208–27.

Roy, Robin E., Kristin S. Weibust, and Carol T. Miller. 2007. "Effects of Stereotypes about Feminists on Feminist Self-identification." *Psychology of Women Quarterly* 31(2): 146–56.

Schnittker, Jason, Jeremy Freese, and Brian Powell. 2003. "Who Are Feminists and What Do They Believe? The Role of Generations." *American Sociological Review* 68(4): 607–22.

Zucker, Alyssa N. 2004. "Disavowing Social Identities: What It Means When Women Say, 'I'm not a feminist, but . . .'" *Psychology of Women Quarterly* 28(4): 423–35.

Chapter 6

An Intersectional Feminist Approach to Quantitative Research

Catherine Harnois

My approach to intersectional feminist research is rooted in what sociologists Maxine Baca Zinn and Bonnie Thornton Dill (1996) term "multiracial feminism." As they describe it, multiracial feminism is a broad-based theoretical perspective in which race, along with gender, class, sexuality, nation, and other systems of inequality are understood to be basic social divisions, structures of power, sites of political struggle, and thus fundamental forces in shaping the lives of all individuals (1996, 324). At the core of multiracial feminism is, first, the recognition that multiple, socially created, intersecting hierarchies "work with and through each other" to organize the world and, second, a strong commitment to challenging these hierarchies.

Baca Zinn and Thornton Dill emphasize that systems of inequality intersect at multiple levels of society. At the individual level, "people experience race, class, gender, and sexuality differently depending upon their social location in the structures of race, class, gender, and sexuality" (326–27). At the interactional level, intersecting systems of inequality guide interpersonal behavior (e.g., friendship networks, patterns of promotion at work, and discrimination and harassment). At the institutional level race, gender, class, and sexuality are each built into our political, economic, educational, and cultural institutions. Whether the focus is the contemporary US criminal justice system or the organization of colleges and universities, it is difficult, if not impossible, to find an institution that can be understood fully based on a single axis of inequality.

Beyond emphasizing the interconnectedness of socially created hierarchies, multiracial feminism emphasizes *relationality*. Relationality, as used in this context, refers to the idea that systems of inequality create not only "differences," but relationships of privilege and oppression. Baca Zinn and

Thornton Dill write, "At the same time that structures of race, class, and gender create disadvantages for women of color, they provide unacknowledged benefits for those who are at the top of these hierarchies—whites, members of the upper classes, and males" (327). The concept of relationality moves us beyond an uncritical "celebrate diversity" framework, by pointing out that rhetoric of "diversity" and "difference" often draws attention away from the oppression and exploitation that have historically constructed these differences.

Finally, multiracial feminism "encompasses wide-ranging methodological approaches, and like other branches of feminist thought, relies on varied theoretical tools" (Baca Zinn and Thornton Dill 1996, 328). As I have argued elsewhere (Harnois 2013), multiracial feminist inquiry is a multivocal project that spans multiple disciplines, including those in the social sciences, but also the arts and humanities; it is a project rooted not only in formal intellectual activity but also in theories developed in the course of activism and politics.

Although it is frequently associated with qualitative and theoretical research, multiracial feminism is also a valuable framework for producing quantitative research. In what follows, I briefly describe how chapter 5, "Who Are Feminists in the United States Today, and What Do They Believe about Social Inequality?" fits within a multiracial feminist framework. I begin situating the overall project within multiracial feminism, and then discuss some of the ways in which multiracial feminism has shaped my analytic approach.

MULTIRACIAL FEMINISM AND
RESEARCH FOR SOCIAL CHANGE

In my day-to-day life, I look around and see gender inequality in the media, in politics, in businesses, religious institutions, universities, the military, and many families too. I watch interactions among colleagues, family members, friends, students, and people I don't know, and I see a lot of behavior that perpetuates not only gender inequality, but other social hierarchies as well: inequalities of race and ethnicity, class, sexuality, age and dis/ability. Other people look at the same organizations and interactions and see something entirely different. How do we explain that?

The question of why some people see high levels of social inequality, to the point of holding an identity based on recognizing and challenging these inequalities, while others don't, is important for social justice work. Quantitative analyses of who feminists are (diverse with respect to race, ethnicity, age, though somewhat more educated than the "average US adult") and what they believe (there's a significant amount of gender, racial, ethnic, and religious inequality, and reducing this inequality is important) provide a more complex picture of US feminism, and can be an important way to challenge stereotypes. Knowledge about who describes themselves as "feminist," and about the broad spectrum of ideas held by feminists, is also valuable for mobilizing feminists and building social justice coalitions. Multiracial feminism provides a valuable theoretical, methodological, and activist framework for thinking about feminist identities in relation to a broad spectrum of social justice issues.

MICROLEVEL INTERSECTIONS

Beyond providing the overall framework for my research question, the insights of multiracial feminism led me to consider the ways in which people's identities and lived experiences shape their relationship to feminism. The idea that systems of inequality work "through one another" at the individual level, that they are "mutually constitutive," means that a person's experiences with gender are always intertwined with the other social statuses they occupy—even for the most privileged among us. No one experiences age apart from gender, for example—even if they themselves reject gender categories—because gender expectations guide interpersonal behavior, and gender continues to organize life at the macro level, in contextually specific ways. In the same way, in a society organized by race, ethnicity, class, and sexuality, these statuses are always to some extent intertwined, though in any particular context one or more statuses may be more salient than others.

To get at the interplay of multiple social statuses I constructed statistical models that allowed potential differences to emerge. In table 5.3, for example, I conducted one analysis for men and women together (model 1), and then ran separate analyses for men (model 3) and women and people identifying with other genders (model 2). By disaggregating the data in this way, I was able to assess whether the characteristics associated with men's describing oneself as more feminist were different from those associated with feminist identity among women and those identifying with another gender. Through this approach, it becomes clear that racial-ethnic identities do not predict the likelihood of claiming a feminist for either of the gender groups considered. This doesn't necessarily mean that the meaning of feminism doesn't vary for these groups. What it means is that, controlling for other variables in the model, people of different racial-ethnic groups, on average, describe themselves as "feminist" at similar levels. On the other hand, among women and those claiming a gender other than man or woman, being a member of the youngest age group (age 18–29) is associated with an increased level of feminist identity. This "age effect" does not seem to predict feminist identities among men, however. Ideally, the analyses might further disaggregate women and those identifying with another gender, though the small number of individuals in this latter category makes this impossible in multivariate models.

In addition to the analyses presented in the chapter, I also investigated the possibility that gender, race, ethnicity, age, and class (using education as a proxy) worked together, in more complex ways, to shape individuals' identities and their beliefs about inequality. I created "interaction terms" to test whether, for example, the positive association between increased educational attainment and strength of feminist identity differed for individuals of different racial-ethnic groups. None were statistically significant, which suggests that the effects of the independent variables are likely similar across the social groups considered in the analyses.

MACROLEVEL INTERSECTIONS

In 2003, Schnittker, Freese, and Powell published an article titled "Who Are Feminists and What Do They Believe?" It is an excellent article and highlights the role of generation in shaping feminist identities. One of the limitations of this article, however, and many others like it, is that it limits the scope of "what feminists believe" to issues dealing explicitly with gender: gender inequality in work and family roles, and support for abortion rights, for example.

In my previous work (Harnois 2005, 2015, 2017), I have argued that multiracial feminism gives us reason to question this gender-centric approach to feminism. As mentioned above, multiracial feminism centralizes the idea that gender, race, class, and other systems of inequality often work "with and through each other," in contextually specific ways (Baca Zinn and Thornton Dill 1996). Systems of inequality do not exist in isolation from each other, but rather mutually shape and reinforce one another. Just as we gain insight into gendered experiences by considering them within the context of intersecting inequalities, I believe there are important insights to gain from considering feminism, and support for gender justice more generally, within this broader context.

This is what I have tried to do here. Rather than focusing exclusively on gender-related beliefs, I have broadened the scope of analysis to include other forms of inequality. Using a multiracial feminist framework, recognizing that for many people issues of gender inequality are intertwined with inequalities of race, ethnicity, religion, class, sexuality, and dis/ability, my analyses ask whether those who identify with feminism are more likely than those who do not to see other forms of social inequality. And the analyses show, with a high degree of confidence, that feminists are in fact more likely to see high levels of a wide range social inequalities.

A BIG PROJECT WITH MANY VOICES

I want to conclude with two larger points from multiracial feminism, which I think are relevant for feminist researchers employing a variety of different methods. First is that multiracial feminism is a huge intellectual and political project that requires many participants, voices, and perspectives. It is highly doubtful that any single study, even a multivolume study, will ever be able to sufficiently capture, with all their contextual nuances, the intersections of all relevant systems of inequality as they occur across time and space. This is true for quantitative and qualitative research. Even when studies are limited to a particular social context, even within a single organization, researchers have to make choices about which aspects of social life to foreground and which to deemphasize, however temporarily.

The second point is that the recognition that all studies provide an incomplete picture of the social world does not undermine the promise or the value of a multiracial feminism or intersectionality. Nor does it mean that all perspectives or analyses are equally valid (Harding 1987; Risman 2001). Instead, acknowledging that all research studies, and indeed all perspectives, are limited in some ways, underscores the importance of conceptualizing multiracial feminist research, like multiracial feminist politics, as an ongoing collective project, requiring multiple voices and multiple approaches. My analysis of contemporary US feminism is limited in a number of ways, but is nonetheless useful, I think, for understanding contemporary US feminism in the context of multiple inequalities.

Something I appreciate most about secondary data analysis projects, such as the one I have included here, is that the data are, in many cases, publicly available and free for anyone who has a computer. As such, they invite alternative analyses and help to increase knowledge of, and dialogue about, a range of social issues. The Survey Documentation and Analysis program has a website where anyone with access to the internet can analyze the 2016 ANES data, as well as data from previous years. Should you want to develop alternative models, by adding variables that you think are important for understanding contemporary feminism, or by examining other variables related to gender and other systems of inequality, you can access the data yourself.[1]

NOTE

1. See http://sda.berkeley.edu/sdaweb/analysis/?dataset=nes2016.

REFERENCES

Baca Zinn, Maxine, and Bonnie Thornton Dill. 1996. "Theorizing Difference from Multiracial Feminism." *Feminist Studies* 22(2): 321–31.

Harding, Sandra G., ed. 1987. *Feminism and Methodology: Social Science Issues.* Bloomington: Indiana University Press.

Harnois, Catherine E. 2005. "Different Paths to Different Feminisms? Bridging Multiracial Feminist Theory and Quantitative Sociological Gender Research." *Gender & Society* 19(6): 809–28.

———. 2013. *Feminist Measures in Survey Research.* Thousand Oaks, CA: Sage.

———. 2015. "Race, Ethnicity, Sexuality, and Women's Political Consciousness of Gender." *Social Psychology Quarterly* 78(4): 365–86.

———. 2017. "Intersectional Masculinities and Gendered Political Consciousness: How Do Race, Ethnicity and Sexuality Shape Men's Awareness of Gender Inequality and Support for Gender Activism?" *Sex Roles* 77(3–4): 141–54.

Risman, Barbara J. 2001. "Calling the Bluff of Value-Free Science." *American Sociological Review* 66(4): 605–11.

Schnittker, Jason, Jeremy Freese, and Brian Powell. 2003. "Who Are Feminists and What Do They Believe? The Role of Generations." *American Sociological Review* 68(4): 607–22.

Chapter 7

Interdependence, Social Inclusion, Poverty, and Family Policy

A Community-Based Exploration

Emily Kane

> The notion of personal responsibility denies the embeddedness of all individuals in the wider society and their reliance on it. It is an image of unfettered individualism—of every man, woman, and child as an island unto themselves. The logic most obviously neglects the "dependency" of children and the fact that no parent is "unfettered." It also neglects the importance, the reality, and the necessity of wider social ties and connections. It makes invisible, in other words, our interdependence. (Hays 2004, 216)

Feminist writers like Hays (2004) criticize the increasing privatization of the family represented in neoliberal US welfare state policies. Poverty researchers note tendencies for public opinion and media representations to focus on individualist and even victim-blaming explanations for US economic outcomes (Merolla, Hunt, and Serpe 2011; Rose and Baumgartner 2013). In this chapter, I present locally anchored, reciprocally engaged research that explores how parents struggling to raise children in poverty and social service providers working with poor families think about personal and social responsibility in relation to family, poverty, and public policy. Though neoliberal narratives may appear to celebrate the potential agency and resilience of parents living in poverty, such attention is deeply misleading if not combined with adequate attention to structural constraints and the way *all* families need social support and resources.

Drawing on interviews grounded in feminist and community-based methods, I argue that providers and parents are constrained by narratives of personal responsibility, but in many ways also recognize interdependence and collective responsibility. The interviews that bring this argument to life, through the words of people with firsthand experience navigating structures related to poverty and family policy, come from two separate projects. One is a set of interviews with participants in a federally funded program called "Family Self-Sufficiency," administered by local public housing authorities throughout the United States.[1] The other is a set of interviews with social service providers who staff a home-visiting program for a child abuse and neglect prevention agency.[2]

BACKGROUND

Two key literatures frame my analysis: feminist and progressive criticism of neoliberal welfare policies, and analyses of public narratives surrounding poverty and wealth. Hays (2004), for example, makes the case that the 1996 "welfare reform" ushered in by the 1996 Personal Responsibility and Work Opportunity Reconciliation Act (PRWORA) combined "two distinct (and contradictory) visions" of work and family that are problematic for all people,[3] but especially so for poor women with children:

> In the Work Plan, work requirements are a way of *rehabilitating* mothers, trans-forming women who would otherwise "merely" stay at home into women who are self-sufficient, independent, productive members of society. The Family Plan, on the other hand, uses work requirements as a way of *punishing* mothers for their failure to get married and stay married . . . the Work Plan follows the logic of classical liberal individualism . . . the Family Plan can be said to follow the logic of a certain form of classical conservatism. (18–19)

Fording, Soss, and Schram (2011, 1611) document a changing policy land-scape in which "programs for poor people have been recast to emphasize behavioral expectations, administrative monitoring, incentives for right behavior, and penalties for noncompliance," and this "sharp turn toward paternalism has intersected with a second development: the reorganization of governance along 'neoliberal' lines." Addressing meager, punitive public assistance programs, with increasingly strict bureaucratic controls, Santiago (2015) counters conservative claims that welfare policies themselves create dependence and further entrench poverty:

> Instead of being sustained by too generous welfare benefits, rising poverty rates in the United States have been fueled by skill-biased technological changes; the globalization of economic and labor markets; declines in union-ization; continued erosion of the U.S. minimum wage; declining progressivity of the federal income tax; and the explosion of executive pay and the size of the financial sector. (3)

But approaches to public assistance that punish and even demonize low-income parents, especially mothers, have become deeply entrenched. As Elliott, Powell, and Brenton (2015) conclude in an interview study with low-income mothers, the dominant ideology "reflects a version of privatized mothering that . . . increases their burdens, stresses, and hardships even while providing a convenient explanation for those very difficulties: *mothers* are to blame. This convenient fiction in turn supports and justifies the huge disparities in life opportunities among American families" (367).

Punitive welfare regimes tend to characterize people living in poverty as passive recipients in need of state control, excluded from the bonds of "mainstream" society, rather than active agents with knowledge, integrity, creativity, and dignity.[4] According to Sykes and colleagues (2015), a notable exception that highlights the damaging effects of other public assistance policies is evident in the Earned Income Tax Credit (EITC). Their interviews with 115 recipients indicate that welfare "benefits are distributed via a stigmatized system in which clients are, by definition, violating social norms of work and self-sufficiency" (259) while

> the way the EITC is targeted and distributed imbues this money with a social meaning: namely, a just reward for work, an opportunity for upward mobility, and a chance to provide recipients' children with some of their "wants" and not just their "needs" . . . creat[ing] feelings of social inclusion and citizenship. (243–44)

My analysis is anchored in literature on poverty and public assistance, but I also draw on literature addressing narratives about poverty more broadly. As Hays (2004) notes, it "makes sense that the demonization of welfare mothers would find a strong foothold in American culture in that it follows smoothly from the ethos of individualism" (125). Public opinion scholars differentiate individualist explanations for poverty (and wealth) from structuralist explanations, with the former attributing variations to individual effort, motivation, or values, and the latter attributing variations to structures like the labor market, educational institutions, tax policy, and other forces beyond individual control. Many in the United States hold both types of beliefs simultaneously, but individualist explanations have become more commonly accepted over time (Santiago 2015). Researchers have also shown that the balance of individual and structural attributions held by respondents varies by their race and class, as well as community-level characteristics like concentrated poverty/disadvantage (Hunt 2004; Merolla, Hunt, and Serpe 2011). Analyses of media representations also document shifts toward individualist beliefs. Just as public opinion scholars argue that such beliefs play a role in crafting the policy climate, media representations may as well.

Media discussion of poverty has shifted from arguments that focus on the structural causes of poverty or the social costs of having large numbers of poor to portrayals of the poor as cheaters and chiselers and of welfare programs doing more harm than good. As the frames have shifted, policies have followed. (Rose and Baumgartner 2013, 22)

DATA AND METHODS

My approach to the qualitative interviews analyzed here is informed by two overlapping methods: feminist and community-based research methods. Hesse-Biber (2014) identifies several commonalities across a range of feminist methods: reflexivity; a focus on lived experience; attention to gender, power, and intersectionality; and social transformation. She notes that feminist research praxis "centralizes the relationship between the researcher and researched to balance differing levels of power and authority" and that "projects seek to study and to redress the many inequities and social injustices that continue to undermine and even destroy the lives of women and their families" (2014, 3).

These commitments resonate with another tradition, community-based research (CBR). Strand and colleagues (2003, 1) highlight three forces pushing US colleges and universities toward community engagement:

Two of them—widespread criticism of higher education's disconnection from communities and growing concern about the professorate's exceedingly narrow definition of research—originated outside the institutions. . . . The third force, recognition of the need to develop students' civic capacity and prepare them for active democratic citizenship, came largely from within the institutions themselves.

Within this context, they advance the particular model of CBR I find compelling, identifying three principles: "collaboration [with community partners]; validation of multiple sources of knowledge and methods of discovery and dissemination; and the goals of social change and social action to achieve social justice" (Strand et al. 2003, 15). Critical attention to the politics of knowledge, and disruption of the hegemony of expert knowledge, is central to the CBR model that Strand and colleagues (2003, 11) advance:

CBR requires acknowledging the validity of local knowledge generated in and through practice in community settings and weighing that alongside institutionalized, scientific and scholarly professional knowledge familiar to faculty and students. Put simply, community-based researchers are interested in . . . how each form of knowledge informs and guides the other.

With these complementary traditions in mind, I have engaged in many local research and action partnerships. Lewiston, its sister city of Auburn, and the surrounding county are located in central Maine, with a population of about 100,000. The area has experienced significant economic challenges as shoe and textile manufacturing began to decline in the 1970s, leaving limited employment opportunities for those with less formal education, as well as limited availability of safe affordable housing, public transportation, and social services. Beginning about fifteen years ago, the area has become home to African-origin refugees, who bring new economic and social opportunity as well as significant need for English-language learning and resettlement services. Lewiston official Phil Nadeau (2011, 55) recognizes the challenges, but also the potential in this particular moment: "The city was well on its way to redefining its economy and, with the arrival of several thousand refugees, reshaping the social landscape while also reversing thirty years of population decline."

Two of my local partnerships are relevant to this chapter, both focused on publicly funded social service provision to families struggling with poverty. Neither partner organization required confidentiality, and the descriptions I offer are adequate to identify them, but I consider it more appropriate not to name the partner organizations explicitly. One organization is our local public housing authority, with whom I partnered to study a Housing and Urban Development (HUD) program; the other is a local child abuse and neglect prevention agency that administers our county's home visiting program.

- *HUD's Family Self-Sufficiency Program (FSS):* This federally funded program allows public housing and Section 8 voucher recipients to set education, employment, and housing goals for increasing their family's "self-sufficiency," and then escrow a portion of their income-indexed rent to be refunded as a lump sum if they reach those goals within a specified period. This program began before the PRWORA radically restructured public assistance to families, but its underlying logic is connected to the 1996 reform that came after it. Our local public housing authority has been administering the program since about 1990, with thirty to forty families participating annually. In the last five years they have done so with new and energetic staffing, along with expanding their services around financial literacy, education, and employment opportunities.
- *Maine Department of Health and Human Services "Maine Families" Home Visiting Program:* Though offering modest services to any family requesting them, primary funding for this program is targeted for families facing significant obstacles. When such families enter the program, a home

visitor is assigned to spend time with them regularly, helping parents access information and support related to pregnancy, infant and child health, nutrition, immunizations, child development, and resources for enhancing the parents' social and economic opportunities. The partner organization's staff includes about twelve home visitors providing services to approximately 130 parents, most with very high needs: 50 percent live on less than $10,000 a year; 35 percent do not have a high school diploma; and the majority have mental health or substance abuse issues. Home visiting programs are available nationwide and funded through a variety of public sources; they are on the list of "evidence-based" practices that the Affordable Care Act identifies as promoting public health.

My ongoing work with each partner included the collection of qualitative interview data addressing mutually designed research questions. For the home visiting program, interviews were conducted with all twelve home visitors during the fall of 2013. For the FSS program, interviews were conducted with eighteen low-income community members who live in public housing or receive Section 8 vouchers, during 2011–2012. Fifteen interviewees were FSS participants; three were potential participants who decided not to enroll. Some topics are not relevant to this chapter's focus, such as a particular emphasis on "Adverse Childhood Experiences" in the home visitor interviews and a particular emphasis on how the housing authority might expand awareness of/participation in the program in the FSS interviews.

The two sets of interviews were connected by their links to my research interests in family, intersectional inequalities, and policy. They were not designed to be analyzed together, but as my separate analyses continued, I came to see clear connections. Both sets of interviews

- emphasize obstacles and opportunities in the lives of low-income families, the role of publicly funded services in addressing those obstacles, and the interplay of individual and structural factors in shaping the experience of poverty in families;
- are framed around cocreating knowledge and validating the expertise of low-income parents and frontline social services providers who interact with them in their homes; and
- address overlapping local problems and engage with academic debates related to those social problems.

The low-income families discussed in each set of interviews face similar but also distinct challenges. The clients discussed in the interviews with home visiting staff are facing even more significant challenges that often include substance abuse, mental health issues, domestic violence histories, and chronic poverty. The public housing interviewees are all parents living in poverty, and most have faced those same challenges at some point. But the process of applying for FSS and setting the goals that program requires means they are, by definition, less significantly challenged at the time of the interviews.

In each project, a semi-structured interview schedule guided the conversations, with about ten general questions, plus probes and follow-ups that asked interviewees to expand on obstacles they perceive, the role of policy, and views on individual and social responsibility for moving families toward more economically secure, safe, and healthy conditions. Across the two projects, the thirty interviewees were all women, and consistent with the demographics of our area, most were white (two participants in each set of interviews were people of color). The home visitors ranged from their early twenties to their sixties, and work with families speaking English, Somali, and Spanish. All have at least bachelor's degrees, typical of publicly funded home visiting programs. The public housing interviewees have a similar age range, with most in their twenties and thirties. Though largely completing some high school to high school diplomas and GEDs, about one-third hold associate's or bachelor's degrees, typically completed during FSS participation.

Interviews were conducted by Bates College students enrolled in two offerings of a seminar on publicly engaged sociology.[5] Interviews lasted about thirty minutes and began with written informed consent following the guidelines of Bates's Institutional Review Board. All participants consented to audio recording and transcription and were ensured confidentiality of their names and identifying details beyond either employment as a home visitor at the partner organization or receipt of local public housing assistance. Home visitor interviews were conducted at their workplace during work hours; therefore no honorarium was offered. A gift basket of treats was brought to the office after the interviews were complete, and preliminary analyses were shared and validated with the home visiting staff. Public housing interviews were conducted in interviewees' homes or private locations on campus or in a public housing site's community center. Through a small grant from Bates's Harward Center for Community Partnerships, we provided participants a modest honorarium of a grocery gift card, the compensation recommended by the public housing officials with whom we partnered.

Ethics are critical in all social research, and especially in reciprocally engaged feminist research. For the home visitor interviews, everyone involved worked to think through the ethics of interviewing employees within their workplace, openly discussing limits to individual confidentiality when we would be sharing results with the home visiting team and their manager. Our topic was directly focused on valuing their knowledge, and through a sustained relationship, an academic collaborator[6] and I know the organization's ethos well. Therefore, we were confident the manager was genuinely interested in their insights, plus home visitors were accustomed to openly discussing the topics we covered in their regular staff meetings. For the public housing interviews, names and identifying information were held strictly confidential, but contact information for potential interview participants was provided by the program administrator; not all of those contacted agreed to participate, but most did.

Verbatim transcriptions were imported into NVivo for data analysis. Following Rubin and Rubin's (2011) guidelines for coding qualitative data, I loosely defined categories based on the literature, and then reviewed material coded into each of those to identify further subdivisions and refinements. Once the general analysis was established, I reread all transcripts, verifying and further refining my analysis to ensure that participants' perspectives were fairly characterized.

BELIEFS ABOUT POVERTY AND RESPONSIBILITY

The balance of individualist and structuralist beliefs about poverty, and emphases on personal and social responsibility, vary across the thirty interviews in some ways that link to the differing circumstances of FSS participants versus the families with whom the home visitors work. In addition, the importance of structural supports is invoked more often by home visitors than by FSS participants, not surprising given that the home visitors are publicly funded to provide just such support. I consider these variations throughout the analysis below. But I also explore similarities in the combination of narratives that privatize the family as the individual responsibility of parents while also attending clearly to structural constraints, social responsibility, and the agency, dignity, and humanity of parents struggling to raise children in poverty. Because the interview questions were not the same in the two sets of interviews, and they were not designed to be combined, I do not offer very specific comparisons of the frequency or intensity with which patterns and contrasts emerge, focusing instead on more general comparisons that flesh out the narratives and perspectives offered by participants.

Individual Explanations and Personal Responsibility

Individualist beliefs about poverty and invocations of personal responsibility were key and often-overlapping code categories, which I defined based on the literatures reviewed previously. Such references appeared in all interviews; when I reread and further coded that material, two interrelated but distinct themes were striking: (1) privatization of the family as the responsibility of parents and (2) dismissive characterizations of individual low-income parents. Both of these were especially common among the FSS participants rather than the home visitors, likely due to differing levels of challenge faced by families connected to the two programs and the role of home visitors as providers of publicly funded family support. All the home visitors referred frequently to individual actions and individual responsibility, and two-thirds at least briefly brought up what sociologists would characterize as "culture of poverty" explanations that situate responsibility within the family rather than broader structural constraints. But only a few made pointedly individualist attributions or suggested that public assistance itself is to blame. For example, one home visitor argued that it is "a vicious cycle" for "families that are linked into the system, it's a very enabling system so it creates dependency," while another noted that "some families, they're just going to do the same thing because that's all they know." When home visitors did invoke these sentiments, they were consistently outweighed by references to social responsibility and social context, as I detail below.

For FSS participants, on the other hand, references to personal responsibility weighed about evenly with references to social responsibility, while individualist and structuralist explanations were both frequently invoked. Again, this is not surprising given the programs to which the two sets of interviewees were linked and their roles as participants versus providers. FSS participants reflected privatized narratives of family by implying that public assistance is supporting parents rather than children. They often used phrases such as "it's your life, you're responsible, period" or "you need to seek out whatever it is you need for yourself," implicitly justifying that poor children should receive support only if their parent(s) take direct responsibility for securing it. Related to that implication was a modal tendency to valorize the "unfettered parent" Hays (2004) notes as mythical. Interviewees were eager to support their children "all on my own," "not to be asking for any help," or "doing everything on my own." Sometimes these references were specifically about public assistance, such as frequent aspirations to be "off the system" or "off the state" or "not needing any help from the government"; one interviewee proclaimed "no more checks from Obama, that would be beautiful." But often these references went beyond public assistance, invoking the even broader vision of "not relying on anyone else." As one parent put it, her goal is "to be independent, literally." Though less direct, some expressions of gratitude for public assistance carried the undercurrent of this personal responsibility narrative, in the hesitance several interviewees felt to offer any structural criticism. One captured it best when noting that her public assistance benefits were so limited that it was very difficult to provide for her children, but then adding: "How rude of me to say that because (the government) helps out so much already and I'm very thankful for what I get . . . don't get me wrong, I feel guilty saying it's their responsibility because in the end it's my responsibility."

FSS participants also criticized other low-income parents, in some cases considering problematic behaviors common (e.g., "for every one that is doing what needs to be done, you have two or three abusing the system" or "most of them I know, they rely more on the government than on themselves"), and in other cases offering a more even balance (e.g., "I've had friends who've taken complete advantage of the government. . . . And then I know people who've been working hard"). The tendency to identify at least some public assistance recipients as "abusing" the system led the majority of FSS interviewees to support time limits and strict bureaucratic controls, often without addressing how children would be supported if their parents were "cut off." As one interviewee put it, "I think the government needs to make that loud and clear. Like at the end of five years, no matter what, that's it. I agree with time restrictions 100 percent." It is understandable that participants in this program focused on self-sufficiency might prefer to distance themselves from the stigmas associated with public assistance, a pattern also consistent with Merolla, Hunt, and Serpe's (2011, 219) analysis of the impact of proximity to poverty on beliefs about its origins:

> Persons living in areas characterized by higher levels of concentrated disadvantage may be afforded more opportunities both for (1) relatively intimate/nonthreatening contact with the poor (e.g., friendships) and (2) myriad undesirable . . . behaviors . . . thus possibly reinforcing both sides of the well-documented "deserving/undeserving poor" dualism in American public opinion.

Structural Explanations and Social Responsibility

These individualist explanations and narratives of personal responsibility for poverty reinforce neoliberal policy regimes unless they are combined with robust attention to structural explanations and robust support for social responsibility and social provision. Both home visitors and FSS interviewees tended to express significant attention to structural explanations, with the FSS interviewees especially likely to do so despite also emphasizing personal responsibility more than the home visitors. And home visitors were especially robust in their support for social responsibility and social provision, partly because of references to their own role as socially supported resources.

Structural Constraints

Home visitors recognized a range of structural constraints in the lives of the families they visit. Almost all mentioned poverty, and more than half specifically noted structures such as lack of access to adequate health care, education, and public transportation plus limited labor markets. A smaller number, several each, brought up food insecurity, low-quality housing stock (especially the effects of lead paint), language barriers, immigration status, and racial and religious discrimination as structural barriers some of their clients face. But FSS interviewees, even in the context of their personal responsibility narratives, mentioned structural constraints more often than home visitors, with the vividness that likely comes from firsthand knowledge. Most often they cited the lack of "good jobs," ones that pay enough to support a family, provide benefits and paid sick days, and offer the dignity and autonomy absent from low-wage service-sector jobs. One interviewee was especially explicit about the degree to which an inadequate labor market explains poverty: "it's not having enough jobs . . . maybe there's 10 percent that just even if you give them a job they're not going to do the work but most of the time, it's going to be 90 percent about not having enough jobs for people to survive."

Linked to these constraints in the labor market, and also emphasized in relation to education and health, interviewees identified lack of affordable, quality child care and transportation options. "If the childcare fails, that's a major issue because what can you do if you don't have the childcare and you're a single mom? You can't make it. And I know a lot of girls out there that they're taking night classes and there's no daycare open and then they can only pay babysitters $1.00 or $2.00 an hour. No one's going to babysit your child for $2.00." In our relatively rural state with hard winters, limited public transportation, and housing options spread out geographically, another interviewee summed up a range of structural constraints: "Daycare's not open until 6:30 and a lot of jobs start at 6:00; what do you do for the extra half hour? Or I've had jobs from 4:00 to 8:00 p.m.; there's no daycare open 4:00 to 8:00 p.m. . . . or if you can't find a job that's in walking distance. . . . I walked in a blizzard a couple times, and I had a jacket but I didn't have mittens, I didn't have a hat. . . . It stinks."[7]

Social Responsibility

The interdependence and collective responsibility that Hays (2004) emphasizes was clearly recognized by most of the FSS interviewees and all the home visitors. Though sometimes limited by the generational poverty narratives expressed by home visitors and the privatized family narratives expressed by FSS interviewees, this recognition of social responsibility and support for public provision to families was frequently noted. For example, one home visitor argued that for people living in poverty,

> The tools that they need to have a better life are just out of reach. Everything they need requires transportation or a checking account or contacts, people who are willing to work with them . . . we come alongside, walking alongside them but being careful to only go the pace they're going.

Another home visitor echoed similar themes and unique angles:

> It takes a full team . . . they have all these problems and you go in and they have no services, the key is to get a group of professionals to be support people around them, because it would be very difficult by yourself, without that support, to even begin to dig yourself out of there.

Home visitors noted support services such as domestic violence shelters, substance abuse and trauma counseling, or basic health and dental care. They expressed respect for public assistance in the form of the Special Supplemental Nutrition Program for Women, Infants, and Children (WIC); the Supplemental Nutrition Program (SNAP); and Temporary Assistance for Needy Families (TANF) and Medicaid, as well as educational, tutoring, and job training programs funded by state or federal governments.

The FSS interviewees also expressed positive views of similar resources, some with gratitude so effusive that it suggested not social responsibility but a more optional form of charity. But most expressed appreciation that implied or stated that everyone needs support and opportunities, especially when surrounded by the structural constraints they recognized well. Some interviewees summed up this perspective succinctly: "it's really good to help families and kids who need it" or "sometimes people need an extra little boost, I am all about helping others." Other interviewees offered more detailed versions of the same argument:

> These programs are there to help people, they're wonderful programs . . . DHS, TANF, the food stamps, MaineCare, the housing authority . . . without it all I would not have been able to do it, it wouldn't have been possible. And now I'm heading into the work force, paying all my state taxes and spending money in the state . . . the government gains from it and people gain from it. That's a win-win.

About half of the FSS interviewees made explicit reference to their desire to see someone else receive publicly funded benefits when they no longer need them: "I've loved the help from MaineCare, from housing, I hope to not have to be part of the programs so that someone else can. I want to be comfortable enough where I don't need the state help. And then someone else can have it so they can get to where they want to be."

DISCUSSION

Given feminist and progressive critiques of the contemporary US welfare state, it is important to underscore the prevalence of individualist narratives in the interview data, while acknowledging the extensive structuralist narratives that more accurately capture structural constraints and the interdependence of all society members. The balance of these narratives in the data I analyze here is at least even, if not weighted toward attention to structural constraints and social responsibility. But I conclude by arguing that the latter attention should be strengthened even more in relation to the individualist elements. That further shift in balance would allow for the remaining emphasis on individuals to highlight the active agency enabled by strong structural supports, rather than devolving into a victim-blaming theory (whether individual or cultural) of poverty and family struggle. The potential in that shift is illustrated by a final interview theme linked to structural explanations and social responsibility: recognition of low-income parents as active agents who want the best for their children, have creative capacities and important knowledge, and should have access to the social inclusion that comes from dignity, respect, and a voice in policy.

Though not viewing low-income parents as political actors, the model used by the agency with whom I partnered on the home visiting interviews defines parents as teachers, acknowledging their expertise and assuming their motivation to raise their children in positive ways. It is a nonpunitive model that treats parents in "at-risk" families as wanting the same things that more economically and socially secure families want, seeking to build reciprocal trust and provide respectful support. One home visitor's comment echoed almost all the others:

> We are very strength-based here and I think that every family loves their child and wants the best for their child . . . they all try and it's not always possible due to education levels and income levels and those things but I think that with us intervening and sharing the resources that we have . . . they all try in one way or another. Whether it's going back to school or working or therapy, they are all doing the best that they can. We all do the best we can with what we've got.

In the FSS interviews, we asked parents what they want for their children and what those children need to know as they grow up, and their responses parallel what Sykes et al. (2015) report in a larger study of low-income parents. They want their children to share in what they see as typically available to more financially secure children: access to educational and occupational opportunities, comfortable housing, and some modest pleasures of consumer culture. When these parents talked about their aspirations to "get off the state" or "not relying on anyone else," most spontaneously mentioned wanting to build up a small savings account. They spoke of emotions they associated with even a small financial cushion: relief, pride, the absence of worry, a sense of self-worth and belonging as they could handle minor emergencies and enjoy treats like taking their children to the beach or out for ice cream. As Sykes and colleagues (2015, 244) document, "stigmatized means-tested programs" of public assistance "create social exclusion, withdrawing a central element of citizenship: social rights standing that comes alongside civic and political rights," while the EITC has what they call "incorporating effects" evident in " the narratives of dignity and dreams" offered by its recipients. The FSS interviewees addressed here also receive more stigmatized forms of public assistance, but the desire for social inclusion, in its economic and cultural aspects, is palpable in their stories. Social inclusion requires adequate material resources, but also a sense of belonging. That sense can flow from perceiving themselves as "not relying on anyone else," the mythical unfettered parent, but could more accurately flow from broad social recognition of "the embeddedness of all individuals in the wider society and their reliance on it" (Hays 2004, 216).

Both social services providers and the general public should be reminded of the reality of structural constraints facing families living in poverty, and reminded of our collective responsibility and interconnectedness. Rather than accepting the false premises of neoliberal welfare policies, we should continue to push back with more progressive theories of social responsibility and the structural foundations of poverty. That is critical at the national level, but also through locally engaged work that brings the expertise of feminist scholars together with the expertise of low-income families and the social services providers who work with them. And along with studying and encouraging the economic and social inclusion enabled by a focus on active agency in the context of structural support, attention should continue to focus on political participation as well.

In the interviews analyzed here, some home visitors referred to the need for expanded public provision, and a few implied that politicians should attend more to the needs of the families with whom they work. Understandably, the model guiding that work, and the focus of the interviews, tended to lead back to household-level solutions. Most of the FSS interviewees focused on that level too, recognizing structural constraints but then emphasizing their own personal responsibility to overcome them. But a handful of those low-income parents offered a more explicitly political analysis of social inequality and social responsibility. One criticized tax policies that allowed manufacturing jobs to be "exported" out of Maine, and another argued that "rich people in their furs" should be pushed to give something up to help level the playing field. A parent living in a nearby rural town said that she has "fought for over a year and a half" to get funded transportation that would allow her teenage daughter to bring her infant son to her high school's day care center, while another interviewee talked about calling her state representative to complain about funding cuts for a program she and her family rely on. "Of course he never called me back, so I'm finding out how I can rally people up, what else I can do." Though this sort of political action and organizing was not a topic we asked about directly in any of the interviews, these instances in which it came up spontaneously are an additional reminder of the agency of low-income parents, and the way their economic, social, and political inclusion carries the potential for social change.

NOTES

1. For more on FSS programs, see Anthony 2005; Theodos et al. 2012.
2. For more on home visiting models, see Azzi-Lessing 2011.
3. Feminist sociologists have criticized US family policy broadly, but I focus on public assistance to low-income families given its relevance here.
4. For recent work emphasizing the agency of the poor, see Barcelos and Gubrium 2014; Santiago 2015. For recent on the role of public assistance workers, see Fording, Soss, and Schram 2011; Watkins-Hayes 2009.
5. See Kane 2012 for details regarding the seminar and CBR projects we pursued.
6. See Davis and Kane 2014.
7. FSS interviewees, in publicly subsidized housing, were protected from some of the unsafe housing conditions faced by home visiting families.

REFERENCES

Anthony, Jerry. 2005. "Family Self-Sufficiency Programs." *Urban Affairs Review* 41: 65–92.

Azzi-Lessing, Lenette. 2011. "Home Visitation Programs." *Early Childhood Research Quarterly* 26: 387–98.

Barcelos, Christie A., and Aline C. Gubrium. 2014. "Reproducing Stories: Strategic Narratives of Teen Pregnancy and Motherhood." *Social Problems* 61: 466–81.

Burawoy, Michael. 2007. "For Public Sociology." In *Public Sociology*, edited by Dan Clawson et al., 23–64. Berkeley: University of California Press.

Clawson, Dan, Robert Zussman, Joya Misra, Naomi Gerstel, Randall Stokes, Douglas Anderton, and Michael Burawoy, eds. 2007. *Public Sociology.* Berkeley: University of California Press.

Davis, Sarah M., and Emily W. Kane. 2014. "Structural Constraints, Family Resilience and Adverse Childhood Experiences." Paper presented at Eastern Sociological Society Annual Meeting, Baltimore, Maryland.

Elliott, Sinikka, Rachel Powell, and Joslyn Brenton. 2015. "Being a Good Mom: Low-Income, Black Single Mothers Negotiate Intensive Mothering." *Journal of Family Issues* 36: 351–70.

Fording, Richard C., Joe Soss, and Sanford F. Schram. 2011. "Race and the Local Politics of Punishment in the New World of Welfare." *American Journal of Sociology* 116: 1610–57.

Hays, Sharon. 2004. *Flat Broke with Children.* New York: Oxford University Press.

Hesse-Biber, Sharlene Nagy, ed. 2014. *Feminist Research Practice: A Primer.* Thousand Oaks, CA: Sage.

Hunt, Matthew O. 2004. "Race/Ethnicity and Beliefs about Wealth and Poverty." *Social Science Quarterly* 85: 827–45.

Kane, Emily W. 2012. "Student Perceptions of Community-Based Research Partners and the Politics of Knowledge." *Michigan Journal of Community Service Learning* 19: 5–16.

Merolla, David M., Matthew O. Hunt, and Richard T. Serpe. 2011. "Concentrated Disadvantage and Beliefs about the Causes of Poverty." *Sociological Perspectives* 54: 205–28.

Nadeau, P. 2011. "A Work in Progress: Lewiston Responds to the Rapid Migration of Somali Refugees." In *Somalis in Maine*, edited by K. A. Huisman, M. Hough, K. M. Langellier, and C. N. Toner, 53–72. Berkeley, CA: North Atlantic Books.

Rose, Max, and Frank R. Baumgartner. 2013. "Framing the Poor." *Policy Studies Journal* 41: 22–53.

Rubin, H., and I. Rubin. 2011. *Qualitative Interviewing.* 3rd ed. Thousand Oaks, CA: Sage.

Santiago, Anna Maria. 2015. "Fifty Years Later: From a War on Poverty to a War on the Poor." *Social Problems* 62: 2–14.

Strand, Kerry J., Nicholas Cutforth, Randy Stoecker, Sam Marullo, and Patrick Donohue. 2003. *Community-Based Research and Higher Education.* San Francisco: Jossey-Bass.

Sykes, Jennifer, Katrin Križ, Kathryn Edin, and Sarah Halpern-Meekin. 2015. "Dignity and Dreams: What the EITC Means to Low-Income Families." *American Sociological Review* 80: 243–67.

Theodos, Brett, Susan J. Popkin, Joe Parilla, and Liza Getsinger. 2012. "The Challenge of Targeting Services." *Social Service Review* 86: 518–38.

Watkins-Hayes, Celeste. 2009. *The New Welfare Bureaucrats.* Chicago: University of Chicago Press.

Chapter 8

Getting to Know People with Experiences and Knowledge Far beyond My Own

Feminism, Public Sociology, and Community-Based Research

Emily Kane

It has been about thirty years since I started graduate school in sociology, inspired by feminist commitments I believed could be advanced by teaching and research as an academic. Twenty-five years into my faculty career, I still believe the academy has a part to play in advancing feminism's many goals, but I have a deeper understanding of obstacles that complicate that potential. This reflection situates the research projects in my empirical chapter by telling the story of how I found myself pursuing them. Gender has always been a central concern in my teaching and scholarship, but it is only in the context of its intersections with inequalities of race, class, sexuality, and nation that I consider gender analysis adequately linked to feminist social change. I believe a wide variety of methods can advance feminist goals, and across my career I have published both quantitative and qualitative work, with data drawn from samples that are international, national, regional, and local. I respect work of various types and across many levels; all are critical to broad understanding and effective action. But over the last ten years, I have gravitated toward the local. The forces shaping that gravity are commitments I have held for a long time, but the labels, and more importantly the communities of discourse that help me articulate and refine them, have shifted over the years. It is at the intersection of three such communities of discourse that I define my current work: feminisms; public sociology; community/civic engagement.

FEMINISMS

Feminist commitments motivated me to study sociology; these commitments are the through-line connecting my work over time. In short, this community of discourse focuses on critical analysis of gender from an intersectional perspective and emphasizes social engagement and activism. Feminist work is anchored in many sites, but feminist research is particularly relevant to this volume. The commonalities across feminist research methods identified by Hesse-Biber (2014, 3), quoted at greater length in my research chapter, are foundational for me too: "reflexivity; a focus on lived experience; attention to gender, power and intersectionality; and social transformation." Over the years I studied public opinion about gender and racial inequalities, because beliefs about inequality have the power to obscure injustice and impede social change. I studied how parents think about childhood gender, because their narratives and the social constraints surrounding parents have the power to reproduce the gender binary and the intersectionally complex heteronormative structures that rely on it. And I am currently studying poverty and family policy, because the narratives and material resource allocation bound up in such policy have the power to harm but also to support women, children, and all society members.

PUBLIC SOCIOLOGY

Within sociology, Sprague (2005, 6) argues that "feminists have made perhaps the most compelling case that conventional practices for the production and distribution of knowledge show patterns of systematic bias that keep sociology from fulfilling its promise." I agree, and have long appreciated the feminist scholars who ask critical questions about epistemology and the political economy of the academy. It is in its resonance with that long-standing work that I came to find Burawoy's (2007) advocacy for "public sociology" a helpful community of discourse. He claims that many sociologies have mutually reinforcing value, but the increasing professionalization of the academy and the discipline tend to push publicly engaged sociology to the sidelines:

> The original passion for social justice . . . that drew so many of us to sociology is channeled into the pursuit of academic credentials. Progress becomes a battery of disciplinary techniques—standardized courses, validated reading lists, bureaucratic rankings, intensive examinations, literature reviews, tailored dissertations, refereed publications, the almighty CV, the job search, the tenure file, and then policing one's colleagues and successors to make sure they all march in step. (24)

In an edited collection advancing and refining Burawoy's call for greater recognition of public sociology, other critical sociologists note the same tendencies.

For many, graduate training resembles something of a shell game—they look under one shell for the public sociology prize that they anticipated; yet when they pick up the shell, nothing is there. The real prizes, they are told, lie under the remaining three shells of professional, policy, and to a lesser extent, critical sociology. (Collins 2007, 103–4)

These articulations of obstacles to public engagement captured something I had felt deeply as I navigated making an academic career and trying to live out the feminist commitments that first motivated me to pursue graduate work in sociology.

COMMUNITY/CIVIC ENGAGEMENT

Beginning around 1995, I delved further into what was then called "service learning," which I consider a powerful teaching tool in general and for sociology in particular. As I collaborated with my college's center for that work (then Center for Service Learning; now the Harward Center for Community Partnerships), I found a new community of discourse that complemented the others and offered new angles to extend them. Within my chapter I quote Strand and colleagues' (2003, 1) analysis of forces shaping US higher education's increasing emphasis on engagement:

Two of them—widespread criticism of higher education's disconnection from communities and growing concern about the professorate's exceedingly narrow definition of research—originated outside the institutions. . . . The third force, recognition of the need to develop students' civic capacity and prepare them for active democratic citizenship, came largely from within the institutions themselves.

These forces overlap with and also diverge from the pressures Burawoy captures in his call for public sociology and are embedded with the trends toward "neoliberal governance" noted in my chapter. One emphasis within this community of discourse that is particularly important to me, and particularly relevant, is reciprocity and the politics of knowledge, also central to feminist research. Saltmarsh and Hartley synthesize trends in the literature on community/civic engagement, calling for democratic epistemology and a "multidirectional flow of knowledge," identifying the "power and politics of expert academic knowledge" as "the core obstacle" to genuine civic engagement (2011, 16). Reciprocal engagement between faculty and students within the academy and the broader communities with which we are interconnected disrupts that power, and thus contributes to more valid and potentially transformative work.

RECIPROCITY AND RESEARCH DESIGN

With these three mutually reinforcing communities of discourse informing my approach, I have struggled to design research projects that simultaneously: (a) contribute to felt needs among local groups concerned with social inequalities; (b) offer feasible opportunities for sociology and gender studies students to learn about topics central to my courses and develop civic capacities; and (c) connect enough to scholarly literatures in my fields that I can not only teach and participate in direct public elements of the work, but also write for a more academic audience. Any one of these objectives would be relatively straightforward to pursue; combining two or especially all three is a struggle worth the effort. Katz-Fishman and Scott (2005), in a critique of Burawoy's approach to public sociology, note that opportunities for connection between academic sociologists and activists or other actors engaged in social change work can come from two "sides": the inside as academics seek new audiences and relevance, or the outside, as social change workers seek new resources for disrupting inequalities. They argue that pressure from outside the academy is where research should be shaped in order to ensure its relevance. The civic engagement movement is generally less progressive in its ambitions than Katz-Fishman and Scott, but it has strong potential for directing the resources of higher education in ways they might appreciate.

Community-based research (CBR) begins with questions arising from communities, and aims to produce research directly relevant to public audiences and the public good. When truly reciprocal, it fosters the kind of work Katz-Fishman and Scott endorse. Though I had been involved in community-engaged learning as a teaching approach for years, in 2007 I introduced the research seminar in which students and I eventually collected the data presented in my chapter. I have taught that seminar five times, and during the first three offerings I also conducted research on student responses to its content and process, which I have subsequently presented and published (Kane 2012). Civically engaged pedagogy, and offering spaces where students' capacities for civic and social action are recognized and further developed while partners' needs are also met, has been satisfying work that I hope contributes to the education of my students and to the public good. In the last few years I have begun to wrap up several research projects that addressed feminist questions but not in partnership with my local communities, and I have wrapped up the research I was conducting on student responses to CBR. So now I find myself in the position to craft the next phase of my work with community needs as the driving factor. I participate in many partnerships that address social inequalities without intersecting with my own specific research interests, such as work on educational inequalities, food insecurity, and the local climate for immigrants and refugees; I look forward to continuing those partnerships. But the projects addressed in my chapter, exploring poverty and family policy through research that foregrounds the lived experiences of low-income parents and social service providers, is for me a step toward balancing the needs of my community partners, my students, and the scholarly literatures within which I hope to contribute.

Students deepen their research and social change skills and enhance their democratic capacities by learning with and from community partners as they cocreate knowledge. Partners move forward in work that crafts new opportunities for families living in poverty. I share what I know from immersion in relevant literatures with people engaged in social change work and have the chance to write reports and papers for public and professional audiences that draw attention to inequalities and advocate policy shifts. And, in a line I borrow from a student in my public sociology seminar (see Kane 2012), I experience the pleasure of "getting to know people with experiences and knowledge far beyond my own."

REFERENCES

Burawoy, Michael. 2007. "For Public Sociology." In *Public Sociology*, edited by Dan Clawson et al., 23–64. Berkeley: University of California Press.

Collins, Patricia Hill. 2007. "Going Public: Doing the Sociology That Had No Name." In *Public Sociology*, edited by Dan Clawson et al., 101–16. Berkeley: University of California Press.

Hesse-Biber, Sharlene Nagy, ed. 2014. *Feminist Research Practice: A Primer*. Thousand Oaks, CA: Sage.

Kane, Emily W. 2012. "Student Perceptions of Community-Based Research Partners and the Politics of Knowledge." *Michigan Journal of Community Service Learning* 19: 5–16.

Katz-Fishman, Walda, and Jerome Scott. 2005. "Comments on Burawoy: A View from the Bottom." *Critical Sociology* 31: 372–74.

Saltmarsh, J., and M. Hartley. 2011. *To Serve a Larger Purpose*. Philadelphia: Temple University Press.

Strand, Kerry J., Nicholas Cutforth, Randy Stoecker, Sam Marullo, and Patrick Donohue. 2003. *Community-Based Research and Higher Education*. San Francisco: Jossey-Bass.

Chapter 9

Maxine Feldman

The Outcast at the Center of the Music

Jo Reger

It is 1969. The woman standing on the stage with her guitar is heavy set with a round face, dark wavy hair and a broad smile. While her body language is tentative and hints at shyness, she pushes forward with the persona of jokester. In this coffee house, an audience has gathered to hear folk music and Maxine Feldman has been on the circuit for years. She cracks jokes and sings their favorites such as "Freight Train" and some Woody Guthrie tunes. Her mood changes though as she looks down at her guitar, gathers her strength and begins to sing her own song.

> I hate not being able to hold my lover's hand
> Except under some dimly lit table.
> Afraid of being who I am.
> I have to tell lies, live in the shadow of fear
> We run half our lives from the damn word "queer."
> It's not your wife that I want,
> It's not your children that I am after.
> It's not my choice that I want to flaunt,
> I just want to hear my lover's laughter.

Her voice is angry and strong, all hints of jokester gone. When she finishes, the room is quiet. It is clear that she is singing about another woman. After a moment, the murmurs of the audience start again. There is no applause. The manager calls to her when she steps off the stage and tells her that she can't keep singing that song. He adds, "Your job is to make them drink and not to make them think." Feldman realizes that she won't be back singing in this coffee house anytime in the future.[1]

The story of Maxine Feldman and her song "Angry Atthis" (Atthis being a lover of Sappho from the isle of Lesbos) could have easily become a forgotten footnote in the history of folk music. However, a confluence of political, social, and cultural factors set the stage for her to play a pivotal role in the development of a social movement community based on music that would become home to thousands of women. Feldman was one of the few folk singers on the circuit in the 1960s who would not hide her sexuality at a time of intense homophobia A self-described "big, loud, Jewish butch lesbian," Feldman, in her later years, recalled how she was blacklisted for straying into the forbidden territory of sexuality and politics. Despite the pain and backlash of these experiences, Feldman kept on singing and her life and music became emblematic of the lesbian-feminist women's music community that existed from the early 1970s until the 1990s. She was so important that novelist Rita Mae Brown placed Feldman in a pivotal scene in the book *In Her Day*. In the novel, the young activist Ilse and Carole, an older apolitical lesbian, meet at a feminist restaurant where Maxine is performing.

> Listening to the singer Maxine Feldman, Carole surveyed the room. The crowd with few exceptions was under thirty and downwardly mobile. . . . Women in the room cheered the singer after she finished a driving song about Marilyn Monroe. Carole wasn't much interested in Marilyn when she was alive much less dead. But a chill swept down her spine. The lyrics reached her. Color rose to her face when she realized she had made some tenuous connection with women as a group. She hadn't realized that, until now, she had believed there were men, women, and herself. (Brown 1988, 18–19)

In this scene, Brown captures how Feldman's music and performances connected women to each other in a space and politicized that experience. At its peak, this women's music community had developed infrastructure of performers, festivals, record labels, and production companies and spread across the United States, with thousands of women participating in performing, producing, and consuming a broad spectrum of music. By the early 1980s, the growth of women's music led one observer to write,

> Only ten years ago, there wasn't a single lesbian-controlled record album. In 1982, there are dozens of such albums available. Concerts are held regularly in all parts of the United States, even in some small cities in conservative regions. Three large annual music festivals attract thousands of women with eight thousand traveling to the remote woods of northern Michigan every August for the Michigan Womyn's Music Festival held there. (Tilchen 1984, 287)

Drawing on archival data, I use Feldman's life story to illustrate how music becomes politicized when filtered through a lens of oppression, prejudice, and discrimination. I begin by discussing how music reflects cultural values.

GENDER, SEXUALITY, AND MUSIC

Scholars argue that music can be an arena or space that exists within a culture and expresses its beliefs and values (Mattern 1998). In societies with discriminatory practices and oppressive ideas, marginalized people are identified and are grouped and treated unequally. These ideas become a part of a culture and are evident in cultural expressions such as in music. Feminist scholars have turned their attention to examining *who* is the unspoken subject of culture and is viewed as the "norm" and *who* is absent and viewed as "other." The subject of culture is then privileged through their invisibility, and all others are marginalized in their absence. One way this operates is identified by Laura Mulvey (1975) in film. She identifies this as the "male gaze," the way in which male domination creates a masculine perspective for all (women and men) who view the object. In this respect, masculine/male becomes the invisible subject fixing feminine/female as the "other" object and defining what the feminine is. Music is similar to film but instead of a gaze from the eye, it is the ear that is gendered. Beverley Diamond notes that "any representation of 'woman' carries the values and belief systems of patriarchal culture" and suggests that people are socialized to hear with a "masculine ear" (Diamond cited in Pegley and Caputo 1994, 298). This is particularly true in popular music. Through the masculine ear, women and men become accustomed to music that describes women as non-adults (i.e., babies, little girls, those in need of love and protection), dangerous women (i.e., barracudas, foxes, evil, bitches, whores), and almost always heterosexual and sexually sought after.

Feminist music scholars have sought to reclaim the musical ear and explore what it means to create feminine, women's and/or feminist music. Acknowledging that not all women experience patriarchy in the same manner, Karen Pegley and Virginia Caputo (1994) argue for a plurality of "feminine ears." One (or more) of these "feminine ears" can be shaped by sexual identity. Suzanne G. Cusick argues that if sexuality is "a way of expressing and/or enacting relations of intimacy through physical pleasures shared, accepted, or given" then "one might expect a significant amount of bleed-through between a person's musicality and a person's sexuality" (1994, 69–70). Lesbians historically have constituted a group in society that is marginalized, and often made absent, in popular culture. According to Cusick, to be a lesbian is to escape the oppression of patriarchy and homophobia creating a musicality that is distinct (1994, 72). In this chapter, I illustrate how Maxine Feldman and others like her helped create a distinct musical ear, which came to be known as "women's music," by refusing to be silenced. Before exploring the dynamics of this, I first detail my methods and data collection.

DATA AND METHODS

The opening scenario is the result of archival research at the Sophia Smith Collection at Smith College as well as an examination of newspapers, magazines, websites, and documentaries. The Smith College Women's Music Archives Collection contains material from 1972 to 2005 in a collection consisting of seventy-nine boxes, approximately seventy-five linear feet of materials. The archives include bibliographies, biographical sketches, clippings, correspondence, newsletters, photographs, posters, publicity materials, song books, sound recordings, videotapes, and memorabilia. I reviewed this material as well as the Boston-produced newspaper *Sojourner* (1975–2002), the magazine *Paid My Dues* (1974–1984), which became *HotWire* magazine (1984–1994), and *Ms.* magazine (from 1972 to 1990). I was also able to locate two related documentaries, *Radical Harmonies* (2002) on the women's music community, and *Lesbiana: A Parallel Revolution* (2012) on lesbian organizing in Canada and the United States. In addition, I reviewed a number of websites focused on Maxine Feldman.[2]

In all, I collected more than 300 documents, which I coded using Dedoose, a qualitative online software program. I gathered these documents in my initial content analysis of the collection using a deductive coding scheme that drew on social movement concepts explaining the rise and decline of social movement communities. These codes were focused on the origins, dissensions, participants, structure, culture, and decline of women's music. The coding became more inductive as I reviewed the documents and began to identify codes related to major performers, issues of community boundaries, and internal debates on race-ethnicity, sexual orientation, disability, social class, sex (men in particular), transgender, and the relationship between feminism and capitalism. I also coded names of organizers, entrepreneurs, organizations, and performers in order to construct a history and to examine how certain prominent people and groups played roles in the community. The music archives also contained several interviews done by the archival historians with performers that I coded paying attention to the development of the community and the ideologies and the construction of a lesbian-feminist identity. Dedoose, similar to other qualitative software, has the ability to code data in multiple ways, as well as give weights that identify the importance of the data to the project. Therefore, I coded data by topic, importance (judged by frequency in the data), and by the date. I then drew upon these codes to construct history, paying particular attention to the origins, development, and decline of the community. It is in that history that I came to realize the importance of Maxine Feldman and the role she played with her song "Angry

Atthis." With the larger history constructed, I narrowed my investigation to the life of Maxine Feldman to investigate how women's music arose.

I chose to focus on archival data to capture the sense of "the present," particularly in the newspaper and magazine stories, meeting minutes, and other correspondence, instead of drawing on interviews that relied on re-membrances of the past. As Shulamit Reinharz notes, documents are cultural artifacts that have the ability to "reflect" conditions of the time and are not affected by the process of study (1992, 147). A content analysis of docu-ments can reveal the difference between remembering a time and place and providing a sense of what it is like to be a participant in the community at the moment. However, it should be noted that this approach has limitations. First, it relies heavily on media stories and the way in which the reporter/writer understood the event being covered or the performer. This became ap-parent in some of the more disparaging coverage from the mainstream press. For example, in a review of the lesbian musician Ferron, Stephen Holden, music critic of the *New York Times*, wrote that "until Ferron, it [women's music] hadn't spawned a songwriter whose lyrics consistently rose above the inspirational versifying that gives so much women's music a pep rally predictability."[3] Second, a researcher is only able to view what was collected and found of value by the archivist. However, these archives contain a variety of documents one would expect to see with few gaps. With these caveats in mind, I now turn to defining women's music.

WHAT IS WOMEN'S MUSIC?

Acknowledging the gendered and sexualized way of hearing and doing music, lesbian feminist musicians argued for the conscious creation of what would come to be called "women's music." Women's music is politicized by its direct confrontation with societal norms that promote misogyny and ho-mophobia. One way that musicians accomplished this was through embrac-ing and valuing the feminine, and the female. One of the pioneers, performer Meg Christian, defined women's music as "music that honors women, that respects our special strengths, celebrates our lives, supports and validates us and teaches us" (Kort 1983 as quoted in Love 2006, 69). Women's music is thereby a conscious and collective valuing of women in opposition to patriar-chy. Scholar Ruth Scovill writes:

> The creation and presentation of Women's Music reflects a consciousness of *women-identification.* Written by and for women, it speaks to their real lives, providing role models and choices that popular music has rarely offered them.

In contrast to popular music's degradation of women, Women's Music holds the feminist and humanist ideals of self-affirmation and mutual support. (1981, 148)

In valuing the women's lives, their differences also became important. Well-known singer Holly Near noted that women's lives, and in particular, lesbian lives are essentially different from men's lives. To her, women's music affirms the uniqueness of women's voices (Love 2006). Women's music then becomes a place where marginalized identities (i.e., woman or lesbian) are made the subject of political discourse. Scholar Nancy Love argues that it is in the creation of this gendered and sexually cognizant music that a political, democratic voice for the marginalized was created. In sum, women's music was more than a cultural phenomenon, but was also the foundation of a community of women united against homophobia, misogyny, and patriarchy, and Maxine Feldman was in the center of it all.

A LIFE IN WOMEN'S MUSIC

A review in 1979 of *Closet Sale*, the only album that Feldman ever released, reads:

> Maxine Feldman began singing by, for, and about women ten years ago. Her first album *Closet Sale* is the culmination of those ten years. Feldman is both sensitive and raucous, angry and bemused, but her lyrics ring of the emotions of the past ten years. Her songs range from blues-jazz in "Objectification" to foot-stomping sing-alongs as in "Bar One."
>
> Perhaps the versatility of her tone is her main strength as she sings of Marilyn Monroe as the ultimate victim one minute, and switches into a stand-up routine the next. Her voice is unmistakable[ly] "Maxine," husky and from the heart, as are the songs. She is soft and restrained in "Bottom Line" and Feldman's best efforts emerge in the lighter comic numbers. The title cut, "Closet Sale," is a gem. Feldman speaks to everyone when she tells of her experience of living as a couple. "You know how tacky we all are when we first get together with someone? We walk through the woods and we find a weed and we get down on our knees and we call it our weed, right?" She has you, and before you know it you're singing along with her "tacky" refrain and wishing it would never end.
>
> Hopefully Maxine this is just the beginning.[4]

The creation of *Closet Sale* was the result of Feldman's lifelong fight to find a way to bring her sexual and gender identity into her music. For a lesbian in the late 1960s, coming out of the closet meant making oneself vulnerable to physical and emotional abuse and economic hardship. Feldman experienced

Photo 9.1. Maxine Feldman in the early years
© 2018 JEB (Joan E. Biren)

a series of homophobic interactions ranging from the larger society, to within the feminist movement, and from those in the women's music community. In addition to shaping her life, each of these experiences played an important role in shaping the origins of the community and the idea of women's music.

Homophobia in Society

In the twenty-first century with same-sex marriage and a visible and active LGBTQ movement, it is important to remember the extreme homophobia faced by anyone suspected of having same-sex romantic feelings. In the late 1950s, Feldman attended Emerson College and was asked to leave in 1961 because of suspicions about her sexuality. Later in an interview, she recalled one of the more painful episodes she had experienced while at Emerson.

> Reporter: Every time there's a blurb written about you or when people introduce you at a concert, they mention two things. One, that you were thrown out of Emerson College for being a dyke and two, that you were taken off the coffee

house circuit in Boston because you "brought around the wrong crowd." Could you fill us in on those two incidents?

Feldman: I was your usual, screwed up, coming out mess. You know how they would have fire drills in dormitories? Well, I was in a room with another woman during a fire drill. So they told me that I had to leave school because I had probably corrupted her. They said I could return after I had psychiatric help for a year, but I didn't feel sick.

An interesting thing happened in my dormitory experience there. I had always known in my heart of hearts that I had been a dyke, a queer. But all of a sudden, rumors started flying in the dormitory that I was a lesbian. People started to avoid me. This was 1962. [My experience] has a lot to do with why I do what I do and what I have done.

During Christmas time in the dorms, I don't know if it holds true for other schools, we put everyone's name in a hat. It was called Secret Santa. You'd do nice things for the person [whose name you drew]. I had someone's name and obviously someone had mine. But nothing had happened in my room except for the very last day. There was this note on my bed. It said, "Go to the drawer, perhaps you'll find more." You know—that kind of thing. So I looked in the drawer and there was another note, which said, "Go to the phone booth in the hallway." Then there was another note. That led to another room, where there was a note attached underneath. . . . Finally it led me to the bathroom medicine cabinet. I opened it up and there was a banana inside with a note on it which said, "I'm sure, as a dyke, you'd know what to do with this."

Now, I had not ever yet slept with another woman (if one wants to look at lesbianism as purely sexual. Certainly in my head I had been with a million women. I had crushes since I was three.) . . .Then, at Emerson, things just progressed from bad to worse. I went to a teacher there who I know was a dyke to talk to her about my feelings. I was just so screwed up. She sent me to the school psychologist. I ran into her years later and I asked her why she did that. She was afraid of losing her job. I understood that, but I refused to accept that as an answer. It was not for me.[5]

This story of her experiences at Emerson demonstrates the level of homophobia in society at this time—a time when a young woman who had not yet had a same-sex relationship or acknowledged her sexuality could be asked to leave a college. At the same time, the fact that the reporter knew of this story illustrates how Feldman's life story had become a part of the discourse of the women's music community and provided a foundation for others' life stories.

Even after her experiences at Emerson and being blacklisted on the folk music circuit, Feldman refused to hide who she was. In the early 1970s, she teamed up with two women who would become important producers in the women's music community, Robin Tyler and Patty Harrison. She met them while working on a degree at El Camino College in Los Angeles (Cullen 2007) and recalled how they brought her into their act.

That was in 1971. Robin Tyler, then of Harrison and Tyler, found me in California on my college campus. They came to play there as a feminist comedy team. I had been trying to bring a feminist consciousness and a lesbian pride consciousness . . . and let me tell you, there was mucho resistance. Anyway, Patty and Robin had come to campus, and they were nervous before going on. So I sang them "Angry Atthis." They said, "We're opening at the Ashgrove next week and you're going to play. Do you know any other songs?" So I whipped together another song and I opened for them and we closed with "Angry Atthis." For six months we played everywhere—once.[6]

Although homophobia had not disappeared, as evidenced by the playing of gigs only once, the gay and lesbian and feminist movements were mobilizing in the 1970s. Feldman's music represented the merging of these two forces, feminism and gay pride, and opportunities for her began to emerge in the creation of women's music. However, even with a women-focused audience, homophobia was still an issue.

HOMOPHOBIA IN FEMINISM

At the same time Feldman was singing "Angry Atthis," Betty Friedan, the president of the National Organization for Women (NOW), was worried about having visible lesbians and lesbian issues as a part of the organization, calling them a "lavender herring" that detracted from women's issues (Echols 1989). While NOW adopted lesbian rights as a part of the mission in 1973, homophobia continued to be an issue in feminist organizations throughout the second wave of feminism (Rupp, Taylor, and Roth, forthcoming). In 1977, Feldman sang at the National Women's conference celebrating International Women's Year. More than 20,000 women gathered to work on ratifying the Equal Rights Amendment and a host of other issues. Later in an interview, Feldman recalled an interaction she had with an older woman at the conference:

A blue haired lady from Austin, Texas came over to me the following day. She said, "I want to talk to you!" And in my mind I said, "Oh shit, here we go again." She said, "You know, I've been working for women's rights for 20 years. I've always thought that you lesbians were ruining things for us." I thought, "Oh no, here comes Lesbian Speech 101." I'm ready to drag out all my information. All my position papers are rolling in my mind. She said, "And yesterday, when you were singing that song 'Amazon,' I looked around to my left and my right and there were women standing up. There were a lot of people who weren't, but there were a lot of people who were standing up and singing with you. It just looked so warm that I got up and put my arm around the woman next to me and we started to sing. All of a sudden, I realized that those other people were going to think that I was a lesbian. It was the first time in my life I realized the kind of fear that you must have and that we've perpetuated on you every single day." She said, "You have changed my position tremendously."[7]

There are two important ideas in this story. First, Feldman changed lives with her music and her willingness to be openly lesbian in her actions and in her performances. Through her work, singing together became a politicizing act that led to new understandings. Second, although the combining of gay rights and feminism offered opportunities to Feldman, homophobia continued.

INTERNALIZED HOMOPHOBIA IN THE COMMUNITY

The homophobia Feldman experienced was not just restricted to feminist meetings and the larger society; as the women's music community began to grow, Feldman experienced others' internalized homophobia in lesbian gatherings as well. Looking back on the early days in women's music, Feldman reflected, "Ironically, I frightened my own kind. Dykes asked, 'Could you tone it down? Why do you have to be so blatant?' I'd say, 'Why do you have to be so closeted? I have to breathe. Anything less than a full breath is deadly.'"[8] She discussed this at length in an interview:

Reporter: One of the things I like most about you is that you are so openly lesbian. Your concerts are a celebration of our identities as lesbians. The first thing out of your mouth is "Give me that old lesbianism."

Feldman: I'm so glad you said that because it's always been my feeling. It's also worked against me. I'm not a "safe" performer. I don't look like the girl next door. When I'm up there people love me. Straight, lesbian, gay. Because I'm telling them the truth as I receive it in a universal tongue. I'm also carrying on the oral tradition of a storyteller. I don't hide anything. I think sometimes even lesbians get very uncomfortable with the really out front thing. I often wonder, perhaps I'm wrong, but I wonder if somewhere deep down they wish that I wasn't quite so blatant or quite so bold. Couldn't she be a little thinner? Couldn't she be a little less Jewish? The excitement for me is when I go up in front of an audience that might not be totally receptive to me and that first moment of truth occurs when the words start to come out and I demand that they sing and say the word with me.[9]

One aspect of the politicization of women's music was not only to address external actions but to also address the ways in which living in a homophobic (as well as fat-phobic and anti-Semitic) society affected women. While women might be willing to hear feminist songs of empowerment, for some, openly addressing their identities as lesbians was difficult. When Feldman released the single of "Angry Atthis" in 1972, she reflected on what it meant to be one of the first to put out a lesbian-oriented record.

> At the end of that version of "Angry Atthis" I didn't say, "No longer afraid of being a lesbian," because a lot of women couldn't say that then. So I sang, "No longer afraid of being who I am." The times were different. I could hardly sell a record with the word "queer" in it.[10]

Feldman's experiences with homophobia in three different contexts—society in general, feminism, and the lesbian-feminist community—illustrate how addressing prejudice and discrimination through music could politicize a community. While Feldman was one of several performers who identified as lesbian, her songs and concerts worked to create space that allowed for a new musical voice to emerge. That voice was one of lesbian and feminist pride, not afraid to identify as someone outside the heterosexual and patriarchal norms, and this lesbian-feminist music community served as a place of safety for thousands of women.

ENDINGS

As the gay and lesbian movement grew over time, the need for the community diminished. In addition, issues of other oppressions such as racism, ethnocentrism, classism, and transphobia were never fully addressed and weakened the community. In 2015, one of the largest and longest-lasting women's music festivals ended. Ironically (or not), this was also the year that the Supreme Court paved the way for same-sex marriage.

Just as Feldman was at the forefront of the women's music community in the 1970s and 1980s, her life also foreshadowed the decline of women's music in the 1990s and early 2000s. While changing cultural beliefs about gays and lesbians brought about more acceptance, the need for the community declined and one issue that all the performers faced was the difficulty in making a living. Feldman had struggled much of her life to make a living as a performer.[11] One way she survived was to continue to do "straight jobs," which were performances where men were in the audience or worked in the field producing a concert, a move that drew criticism from those who advocated lesbian separatism.[12] For example, in 1977 Feldman reflected on her career in response to the question, "How do you feel about your own music as part of women's music, as business and as culture?"

That's a real difficult question since none of the women's companies want to record me. Since I've been around a long time and there has been no offering, I'm not sure. Yet I see my audience responding, so what choice does that leave me? A) recording myself and trying to gather the money which I don't have, or B) finding a small male-owned independent company. . . . I don't have the finances so that leaves me in a bind. If I use men on my album people are gonna trash me. But what am I supposed to do? Ask my sisters to work for free? I can't do that.[13]

A sad note at the end of her 1980 interview in the *Gay Community News* is telling of how her financial problems continued. It reads:

During the rainy weekend of the March on Washington for Lesbian and Gay Rights, Maxine slipped on some wet stage steps. Her guitar, a Martin, was fatally damaged. Since then, she has had to use borrowed guitars. If anyone would like to contribute a Martin guitar to Maxine or help her get one, please contact her through Galaxia Records, P.O. Box 212, Woburn, MA 01801.[14]

Maxine Feldman died on August 17, 2007, at the age of sixty-two. To the end, Feldman was a pioneer adopting a gender-fluid identity. According to singer Jamie Anderson:

Comfortable with either gender pronoun, s/he confided to friends that s/he was too old for surgery and comfortable in her/his body. S/he passed away in Albuquerque of natural causes on August 17, and is survived by her/his partner Helen Thornton. All of us who are gay, lesbian, bi or transsexual stand on his/her strong shoulders.[15]

In sum, Maxine Feldman was a politicizing force that made music central to a community embracing feminist and lesbian pride. Her life experiences illustrate the forces that created a collectivity and a new musical ear. It seems fitting to end with the philosophy that drove Feldman to seek a world where all identities were accepted and embraced. S/he said in an interview in the early years of the community, "I want the world. I want everything. I want the whole cake, no crumbs. I'm tired of crumbs. I want the whole cake."[16]

NOTES

1. "Women's Music Politics for Sale," *Gay Community News Music Supplement*, n.d., 1–5, 8, 12. Series I, Box 1, File 7, Women's Music Archives, Sophia Smith Collection, Smith College [Document 17].

2. Those include Jewish Women's Archives, wa.org/weremember/feldman-maxine; YouTube, https://www.youtube.com/watch?v=udz8IiJExaE; Spiral Goddess, http://

www.spiralgoddess.com/MaxineFeldman.html; Queer Music Heritage, http://www
.queermusicheritage.com/apr2002.html; and Discogs, http://www.discogs.com/Maxine
-Feldman-Closet-Sale/release/1644562.

3. Stephen Holden, "'Women's Music': Debut by Ferron," *New York Times*, October 22, 1982, http://www.nytimes.com/1982/10/22/arts/women-s-music-debut-by
-ferron.html.

4. Anne Rush, "Feldman's Follies," *Sojourner*, December 1979, 22, Women's Music Archives, Sophia Smith Collection, Smith College [Document 130A].

5. "Maxine Feldman," *Gay Community News*, April 19, 1980, no pp., Series 1, Box 1, Folder—Clippings 1980. Women's Music Archives, Sophia Smith Collection, Smith College [Document 175].

6. "Maxine Feldman," *Gay Community News*.

7. "Maxine Feldman," *Gay Community News*.

8. "Maxine Feldman: The Original Amazon Woman Rising," *Sojourner*, February 1995, 14–15, Series II, Box 3, Folder—Maxine Feldman. Women's Music Archives, Sophia Smith Collection, Smith College [Document 190].

9. "Maxine Feldman," *Gay Community News*.

10. "Maxine Feldman," *Gay Community News*.

11. "How Feminist Musicians Keep Going," *Sojourner*, January 1986, Series II, Box 3, Folder—Alix Dobkin. Women's Music Archives, Sophia Smith Collection, Smith College [Document 181].

12. "Maxine Feldman," *Gay Community News*.

13. Karen Corti and Toni L. Armstrong, "A Sometimes Serious Person: An Interview with Maxine Feldman," *Paid My Dues* II(1), Fall 1977: 26–17, 39 [Document 272].

14. "Maxine Feldman," *Gay Community News*.

15. Jamie Anderson, "Maxine Feldman: Folk Musician, Lesbian Activist," Jewish Women's Archive, http://jwa.org/weremember/feldman-maxine. First published in http://www.singout.org/magazine.html.

16. Corti and Armstrong, "A Sometimes Serious Person."

REFERENCES

Brown, Rita Mae. 1988. *In Her Day.* New York: Bantam Books.

Cullen, Frank. 2007. "Maxine Feldman." In *Vaudeville, Old & New: An Encyclopedia of Variety Performers in America*, edited by Frank Cullen with Florence Hackman and Donald McNeilly, 372–75. New York: Routledge.

Cusick, Suzanne G. 1994. "On a Lesbian Relationship with Music: A Serious Effort Not to Think Straight." In *Queering the Pitch: The New Gay and Lesbian Musicology*, edited by Philip Brett, Elizabeth Wood, and Gary C. Thomas, 67–83. New York: Routledge.

Echols, Alice. 1989. *Daring to Be Bad: Radical Feminism in America, 1967–1975.* Minneapolis: University of Minnesota Press.

Kort, Michelle. 1983. "Sisterhood Is Profitable," *Mother Jones*, July 1983, 39–44.

Love, Nancy S. 2006. *Musical Democracy*. New York: State University of New York Press.

Mattern, Mark. 1998. *Acting in Concert: Music, Community and Political Action*. New Brunswick, NJ: Rutgers University Press.

Mulvey, Laura. 1975. "Visual Pleasure and Narrative Cinema." *Screen* 16(3): 6–18.

Pegley, Karen, and Virginia Caputo. 1994. "Growing Up Female(s): Retrospective Thought on Musical Preferences and Meanings." In *Queering the Pitch: The New Gay and Lesbian Musicology*, edited by Philip Brett, Elizabeth Wood, and Gary C. Thomas, 297–314. New York: Routledge.

Scovill, Ruth. 1981. "Women's Music." In *Women's Culture: The Women's Renaissance of the Seventies*, edited by Gayle Kimball, 148–62. Metuchen, NJ: Scarecrow Press.

Reinharz, Shulamit. 1992. *Feminist Methods in Social Research*. New York: Oxford University Press.

Rupp, Leila J., Verta Taylor, and Benita Roth. Forthcoming. "Women in the Lesbian, Gay, Bisexual, and Transgender Movement." In *The Oxford Handbook of U.S. Women's Social Movement Activism*, edited by Holly McCammon, Lee Ann Banaszak, Verta Taylor, and Jo Reger. New York: Oxford University Press.

Tilchen, Maida. 1984. "Lesbians and Women's Music." In *Women-Identified Women*, edited by Trudy Darty and Sandee Potter, 287–303. New York: Mayfield Publishing.

Chapter 10

What's So Feminist about Archival Research?

Jo Reger

I became a part of a thriving women's community in the mid-1980s and attended women-only dances, went to womyn's (the spelling of the time) music festivals, and volunteered my time at a feminist bookstore. In many ways, those were some of the most satisfying years of my life, being embedded in a rich and vibrant community of feminist activists, and those years shaped who I am now as a feminist researcher. I don't think I ever heard Maxine Feldman sing; if I did, it did not register with me. However, when I found her story in the archives of the Sophia Smith collection on women's music, I was instantly taken with her. Through the archives at Smith College and then in feminist journals, newspapers and magazines, videos, books, and other materials, I searched for everything I could find on Maxine Feldman.

As I did, I began an interaction with her, a sort of dialogue across time and space. Her side of the interaction was her honesty in the interviews she did where she spoke about the hurts, slights, and joys she experienced in her life. My side of the conversation was to be conscious of my emotions as I gathered pieces of her story. When I felt in awe by her actions, it led me to think of her role as a pioneer in women's music. When I winced at the corny jokes, I could then see how she played the court jester to moderate the radical nature of her message, even amid the community she helped create. When she came across as petulant or hurt in an interview, I could see how difficult it must have been to be a pioneer and then see how others, who came after her, succeeded in ways she did not. By focusing on my emotions, a dialogue of sorts was constructed that pushed my understanding of her role in this community.

Feminist scholars have long argued that the emotional and the intellectual are not binaries but are linked (Jaggar 1989) and belong in research (Kleinman and Copp 1993). As I continue to grow as a researcher, I have begun to

97

use my emotions more and more in my research. One of my early publications traced a "failed" participant observation of a feminist bookstore and the way it felt to uncoil some of the lessons I had learned about scientific objectivity (Reger 2001). More recently, I attended a "slut walk" and drew on my emotions to construct an auto-ethnography of the protest and the issues of contemporary feminism (Reger 2015). In this project, I drew on my feelings as a participant to think through some of the debates of contemporary feminism. Turning to archival work for this project, I did not expect emotions to be relevant. However, one of the most profound lessons I have learned in doing research is to listen to what feminist researchers Sherryl Kleinman and Martha A. Copp call "twinges" or "troubling feelings" (1993, 56). They argue that these feelings often tell researchers when something important is being submerged or ignored, and needs to be examined. To engage in this process is to be reflexive, a key component of any feminist research that continually examines the assumptions that are being made and circles back to the source for verification. Using emotions in a reflexive manner is to examine your emotions and responses as a researcher and then to return to your data to see what is revealed.

A key example of these "twinges" becoming reflexive moments shaping research is when I found the words to "Angry Atthis." I was intrigued by Feldman at this point, and by the courage it took to sing that song at a time when there was virtually no space for an open lesbian identity in society. However, I have to admit that while I found the lyrics engaging, I dismissed the music as "soft" and "overly impassioned" folk music. Then I found a recording of her singing it. It is not soft or overly impassioned but instead strong, bold, and angry. The shame I felt for misjudging her importance made me realize that I had also bought into the idea that "women's music" was trite, overly emotional, and politically unimportant. It was then that I could see more clearly how this community was both marginalized and politicized in the creation of music that affirmed a lesbian-feminist identity.

While working on this chapter, I had a conversation with an emerging scholar struggling with her emotions as she did interviews in the field. As we talked, I realized that there is a systematic way to approach the process of emotional reflection, but it has taken me a long time to begin to articulate my process of doing so. I have come to realize that the key to using emotions in research is to be able gather data, in this case documents, and then to make space to reflect on that process (and here I mean the process of gathering the data). One way to do this is through journaling. I have used those black-and-white composition notebooks as research journals for most of my career. For me, the process of writing in a notebook is one that allows me to reflect. Many qualitative research guides encourage scholars to write a variety of memos as they gather data. For emotional reflexivity, I write memos where I don't try to synthesize or theoretically situate the data, but instead just allow myself to note my reactions to the data gathered or sorted that day. I ask myself, "What have I been thinking and feeling as I worked today?"

What makes it feminist is the next step. For some scholars, these moments of reflection are enough to clear the mind and allow the process of data collection to continue. For feminist researchers, journaling should be just the beginning. The next step is to go back and identify the source of emotions. In my reflection on the song "Angry Atthis," I identified the feeling of shame. Shame is an emotion that emerges from doing something you are not supposed to do, something you feel guilty about. I felt the twinge of shame for judging and dismissing her music too quickly. I realized that the root of that dismissal was an acceptance of a mainstream view of women's music as trite and overly sentimental. When I could recognize this bias, I could see more clearly the depth of her contribution to the creation of women's music. As a result, I was able to delve deeper into the data and I began to connect sources into a narrative of her importance. One example is tracking down the Rita Mae Brown novel that describes one of her performances. Because of this process, what could have been a sentence in an article or chapter—"Maxine Feldman was one of the pioneers of women's music but did not achieve much success in her career"—became a focal point of the empirical and theoretical story of the women's music community.

I think it is important to note that some of the more obvious emotions were not necessarily the most helpful. Here I distinguish between emotional "twinges," those emotions that are identified through a system of reflection and emotional feedback, the immediate feeling that comes from finding disturbing data. For example, the amount of homophobia that Feldman experienced in every aspect of her life was breathtaking in scope and infuriating. But I find that focusing on this level of emotion can often block me from going deeper into the data. By focusing on the all-too-available emotions of anger at her treatment at Emerson College, by feminists and by other lesbians, it is too easy to view Feldman as a victim. By delving into "Angry Atthis" (which itself is a statement of emotion), I was able to see Feldman as more than a victim, as a pioneer who helped create a community.

In closing, I argue that archival research can be feminist for a myriad of reasons. First, this research is very much connected to my life history. Feminist research does not have to be removed from the researcher to be worthy of consideration. Indeed, many feminist scholars argue that all research is influenced by the positionality of the researcher. Acknowledging my connection to this research allows me to move deeper into my analysis. Second, knowing that I am a part of the process allows me to examine my emotions and, as I have argued, construct a more complex framework for understanding this community and its origins, struggles, failures, and victories. Through the acknowledgment of positionality and emotion, all research methods can be feminist research methods—even when you are speaking with those who are no longer with us through the emotional lens of an archival document.

REFERENCES

Jaggar, Alison M. 1989. "Love & Knowledge: Emotion in Feminist Epistemology." In *Gender/Body/Knowledge: Feminist Reconstructions of Being and Knowing*, edited by A. M. Jaggar and S. R. Bordo, 145–71. New Brunswick, NJ: Rutgers University Press.

Kleinman, Sherryl, and Martha A. Copp. 1993. *Emotions and Fieldwork*. Newbury Park, CA: Sage.

Reger, Jo. 2001. "Emotions, Objectivity and Voice: An Analysis of a 'Failed' Participant Observation." *Women's Studies International Forum* 24/25: 605–16.

———. 2015. "The Story of a Slut Walk: Sexuality, Race and Generational Divisions in Contemporary Feminist Activism." *Journal of Contemporary Ethnography* 44 (1): 84–112.

Chapter 11

Does Science Do More Harm Than Good?

A Mixed-Methods Analysis of African American Women's Attitudes toward Science

Maura Kelly, Gordon Gauchat, Katie Acosta,
Elizabeth Withers, and Joyce McNair

Continuing advances in medical technology, information communication, and bioengineering, coupled with aging populations, the risk of global pandemics, and the long-term consequences of climate change, suggest that scientific knowledge will only grow in its significance to every aspect of social life. Even so, research on public perceptions of science has been slow to develop theory that addresses the impact of power and culture on these attitudes as well as theory that conceptualizes a variety of audiences or publics with unique relationships to science as culture and as an enterprise (Bauer, Allum, and Miller 2007; Miller 2004). Taking an intersectional perspective, it is critical to understand how people at unique intersections of race and gender experience and understand science. In this analysis, we examine African American women's attitudes toward science, using a mixed-methods approach. We draw on quantitative survey data representative of the US population to assess how men and women who are African American and white understand science. In addition, we draw on qualitative interviews with African American women in Portland, Oregon, to further contextualize how the lived experiences at the intersection of race and gender inform perceptions of science. We focus on African American women because they have heightened experiences of exclusion and mistrust of science, based on both their race and gender (Hanson 2009; Perry et al. 2012).

Early research on public attitudes toward science suggested that science has little cultural meaning to those who lacked sufficient *scientific knowledge*—here meaning fact-like information about scientific methods, developments, and basic vocabulary (Miller 2004). In research, scientific knowledge can be operationalized as years of education, number of science classes, and/or correctly answering factual questions about science (i.e., a "science quiz").

Recent work in sociology has pointed to the importance of multiple modes of knowledge, including political identities, religious views, and belief systems that comingle and compete with scientific knowledge, producing divided views on what science is, what it should do, and whether it has net positive effects on society (Gauchat 2011, 2012; Gauchat and Andrews 2018). Cognitively, people draw on available modes of knowledge to develop general dispositions or schemata that shape their subsequent behaviors and beliefs, rather than carefully search out and deliberate over the relevant information (DiMaggio 1997; Vaisey 2009).

Past research has demonstrated that the public's attitudes toward science vary by both race and gender, although these identities are rarely the focus of research on this topic. Overall, white respondents report more favorable attitudes about science than do people of color (Gauchat 2011). White respondents also report more confidence in scientific knowledge than do African Americans (Plutzer 2013). While research on trust in science among African Americans is underdeveloped, trust has received considerably more attention in the area of race and medicine. Scholars have considered the historical and ongoing reasons for mistrust of medical providers, health-care institutions, and medical research (Scharff et al. 2010; Westergaard et al. 2014). For example, in focus groups with African Americans, Darcell P. Scharff and his colleagues (2010) found that mistrust of the health-care system has led to significant barriers to African Americans' participation in medical research. This mistrust is based on historical discrimination (e.g., the Tuskegee syphilis experiment) and ongoing discrimination in the health-care system (Scharff et al. 2010). Too often, research assessing issues of trust uses race as a control variable without any systematic assessment of the root causes of the disparities yielded in the study findings. These same works may acknowledge that racial discrimination drives this distrust; however, they lack an intersectional analysis of how levels of trust are shaped by race, gender, and class.

Research also suggests that women hold less positive views of science than men, which scholars attribute to women's lower levels of scientific knowledge, lower overall educational attainment, stronger religious views, and lower levels of trust in science (Elder, Greene, and Lizotte 2018; Hayes and Tariq 2000; Sturgis and Allum 2001). For example, one recent study found that women (and also people of color) were more skeptical than men of genetically modified foods (Elder, Greene, and Lizotte 2018). Relatively little is known specifically about African American women and science. Previous research on this topic has primarily focused on African American girls in educational contexts (e.g., Hanson 2009; Perry et al. 2012). Overall, there is a significant amount of scholarship on women and science, given recent attention to women in STEM (science, technology, engineering, and math) from scholars, educators, and policy makers; however, less is known about women's attitudes toward science across a variety of contexts.

In sum, previous research has not fully explained how different publics' experiences of the social world, rooted in social locations and historical relationships to power, shape more complex cultural understandings of science. This research contributes an improved theoretical approach to studying public perceptions in marginalized groups by examining the intersection of race and gender, and integrating the cultural and cognitive aspects of public perceptions into our approach.

DATA AND METHODS

In order to assess how race and gender shape African American women's attitudes toward science, we adopted a mixed-methods approach. We first examined nationally representative survey data to understand the broad trends in race, gender, and attitudes toward science. We then conducted a study of ten qualitative interviews to provide a more nuanced understanding of African American women's attitudes toward science.

Quantitative Data

For this study, data from the 2008 and 2010 survey years of the General Social Survey (GSS) were pooled for analysis because both years included the key survey question, which asks respondents how much they agree or disagree with the statement: "Overall, modern science does more harm than good." We excluded those respondents who had missing values for this variable from our analytic sample. Additionally, we focused our analyses on the difference in opinions between African American women, African American men, white women, and white men. As such, the analytic sample includes only those respondents who report being African American/Black (any ethnicity) or non-Hispanic white (excluding all other racial/ethnic minority groups). Missing cases from the remaining independent variables were excluded from analyses, giving us the final analytic sample of N = 2,006.

Our outcome variable measures respondents' attitudes toward science by asking how much they agree with the statement: "Overall, modern science does more harm than good." Responses were provided via a five-point Likert scale from strongly agree (coded 1) to strongly disagree (coded 5). Our primary interest was to estimate the influence of race and gender on attitudes toward science. In order to capture the intersection of race and gender, we combined the measures of race and gender to create four new mutually exclusive variables (white men, white women, African American men, African American women).

We included several variables that might affect respondents' attitudes toward science. First, we included socioeconomic variables measuring age and income. A continuous measure of age was also used in the analysis (top-coded at 89 for those age 89 or older). The income variable is a categorical measure of respondents' total family income from the previous year. The income variable was converted to real dollars using the midpoint from each category. For example, if a respondent reported earning $4,000 to $4,999 in total family income, their response was recoded as $4,500. For the highest earners, 30 percent was added to the lower limit of the top category ($25,000 + 30% = $32,500).

We also included variables for education, religiosity, and political views. The education variable is a continuous measure of the highest year of school completed by the respondent (coded 0–20). Religiosity was measured using a survey measure that asked, "To what extent do you consider yourself a religious person? Are you . . ." Respondents chose from the following answers: Very religious (coded 1), Moderately religious (coded 2), Slightly religious (coded 3), and Not religious (coded 4). The question on political party affiliation asked respondents, "Generally speaking, do you usually think of yourself as a Republican, Democrat, Independent, or what?" Respondents chose from the following categories: Strong Democrat, Not strong Democrat, Independent near Democrat, Independent, Independent near Republican, Not strong Republican, Strong Republican, and Other party. For our analysis we recoded the variable into three separate dichotomous measures, Democrat, Independent, and Republican. Those who responded belonging to an "Other party" were included in the Independent measure.

Qualitative Data

The qualitative component of this study consisted of interviews with ten African American women in Portland, Oregon (located in the Pacific Northwest region of the United States). Participants for the qualitative interviews were recruited from two historically African American neighborhoods in North Portland (Kenton and Piedmont). In order to be eligible to participate, participants had to be at least eighteen years of age and identify as an African American woman. Flyers for the study were posted in a variety of places in the North Portland neighborhoods: Portland Community College (PCC) Cascade campus, two public library branches, and local businesses. The women's resource center at PCC recommended several participants in an effort to assist the study. Additional participants were recruited using snowball sampling, that is, initial participants referred others who met the criteria for the study.

These participants are not intended to be representative of all African American women; rather, we draw on this convenience sample to understand how race and gender can impact attitudes toward science.

Interviews took place in a study room located at the library of the PCC campus in November and December 2014. The interviews lasted an average of thirty-nine minutes and were audio-recorded and fully transcribed. For their willingness to participate in the study, participants were given a $20 gift card. Interviews were conducted by Joyce McNair, an African American female sociology graduate student at Portland State. Participants spoke openly about issues of race and racism as well as gender and sexism in a manner that they may not have with a white and/or male researcher.

The respondents ranged in age from nineteen to seventy-nine years and in social class from self-identified "low income" to "middle class" (see table 11.1). Participants had a range of relationship statuses. Six participants had children. All participants had graduated from high school. Two participants had received bachelor's degrees and an additional four participants were pursuing degrees at the community college branch where recruitment occurred. Nine of ten participants reported their political party affiliation as Democrat (one participant identified as an Independent with slightly liberal views).[1] All of our participants identified as Christian. All names are pseudonyms and identifying information has been excluded to protect confidentiality.

Interviews were semi-structured in style. Initial questions were drawn from previously used survey items. For example, the first question on the interview guide was "Overall, modern science does more harm than good. Do you agree or disagree?" Participants were asked follow-up questions, or probes, about why they felt the way they did. They were also specifically asked how their race and gender and social class shaped their attitudes toward science.[2] After the broad questions on science, participants were asked about some specific science controversies: vaccines, inequality, and global warming. Participants were next asked questions about how they get their information about science, including questions about their experiences with math and science courses in school. At the end of the interview, the interviewer administered a twelve-question version of a "science quiz" used in previous surveys to assess participants' scientific literacy. Our participants' scores on the science quiz varied widely, with several participants getting only a few questions correct and two participants receiving perfect scores.

We analyzed the interview data with the assistance of the qualitative coding software Dedoose. We first coded for theoretically important themes identified in previous research as well as emerging themes in our data related to race, gender, and attitudes toward science. We then compared the findings of the qualitative data to the findings from the quantitative

Table 11.1. Demographics of Interview Sample

Pseudonym	Age	Relationship Status	Kids	Education	Political Party	Religion	Science Quiz
April	21	Single	0	High school, some college (currently attending)	Democrat	Catholic	67
Araminta	22	Single	0	High school, some college (currently attending)	Democrat	Christian	100
Autumn	79	Widow	3	High school	Democrat	Protestant	8
Brooklyn	25	Single	0	Bachelor's	Independent	Protestant	100
Caitlin	19	Single	0	High school, some college (currently attending)	Democrat	Protestant	25
Emery	61	Single	1	High school, medical assistant degree	Democrat	Baptist	75
Gloria	63	Married	4	High school, beauty school	Democrat	Baptist	58
Jet	63	Divorced	4	Bachelor's	Democrat	Christian	33
London	24	Single	1	High school, some college	Democrat	Christian	33
McKenzie	45	Married	4	High school, some college (currently attending)	Democrat	Church of God and Christ	67

analysis. We refined the themes we had identified in the qualitative data to develop a cohesive and complementary narrative across both the qualitative and quantitative data. The themes addressed in the qualitative data include defining science, benefits and harms of science, lack of knowledge about science and perceived exclusion from science, and impact of political and religious views on attitudes toward science.

Analytic Strategy

This study took a sequential approach to mixed-methods in which we began with a quantitative preliminary input, followed by a qualitative core analysis (Morgan 2014). Specifically, we first assessed attitudes toward science among white and African American men and women using the GSS data. This analysis focuses on the survey item: "Overall, modern science does more harm than good. Do you agree or disagree?" First, descriptive cross-tabulations were conducted to examine the relationships between variables and across race/gender categories. Next, linear regression analysis was conducted to examine the relationship between race and gender and attitudes toward the value of science. The first model examined the relationship between our primary independent variables (race/gender groups) and the dependent variable (attitudes toward science). The second model added all of the other variables to identify additional predictors of attitudes toward science.

After identifying the attitudes toward science of African American women in the GSS data, we turned to interviews to get a more in-depth understanding of how participants engage with questions about science. We began the interviews with the exact wording of the survey questions. From the open-ended responses in the interviews, we were able to identify what aspects of science were at the forefront of participants' minds when they answered these questions. Further, we probed our interview participants to learn why they answered these questions the way they did and how they viewed their race and gender identities as relevant to these topics. Taken together, the quantitative and qualitative data allow us to understand both the broad trends in African American women's attitudes toward science and an in-depth understanding of the experiences and knowledge leading to those attitudes. For this study, we chose to focus on a single intersection of race and gender in order to provide maximum depth to our analysis.

QUANTITATIVE FINDINGS

The first step in our analysis was to look at the key variables and note any difference across the four race/gender groups: white men, white women,

African American men, African American women (see table 11.2). As shown in the first row of table 11.2, white men had the *highest* average response to the item "Science does more harm than good," indicating that white men had the *most positive* views on science, followed by white women and African American men, with African American women reporting the most negative views on science. In further analysis (not shown), we found that African American women's views toward science were significantly different from white women as well as white men (but were *not* significantly different from African American men).

Table 11.2 also describes several other differences between the four gender/race groups: age (African American men and African American women were slightly younger than white men; white women were slightly older than white men), family income (white men had higher family income than all other race/gender groups), education (African Americans had lower levels of educational attainment that whites), religiosity (African American women reported being the most religious, followed by African American men and white women, with white men being the least religious), and political party (African Americans were much more likely to identify as Democrats than whites; white women were somewhat more likely to identify as Democrats than white men).

We then turned to look at a regression analysis to understand what other factors are related to attitudes toward science (table 11.3). Model 1 shows a regression of the four race/gender groups (white men are the reference category) on the item "Science does more harm than good." The coefficients for white women, African American men, and African American women are all *negative* in model 1, meaning that these race/gender groups are *more likely to agree* with the statement "science does more harm than good," compared to white men. Thus, consistent with findings shown in table 11.2, we see that African American women have the most negative views on science, followed by African American men, white women, and white men.

In model 2, we added in key demographic variables, including factors that are known to shape attitudes toward science from previous research. Here, we see that several factors are associated with more positive attitudes toward science: higher education, being a Democrat (in comparison to being a Republican), and being less religious. Notably, a few variables were not significant predictors of attitudes toward science: age, income, and being an Independent (in comparison to being a Republican). In model 2, the coefficients for our race/gender groups (white women, African American men, and African American women) have gotten smaller but are still statistically significant. This means that the additional factors we added into model 2 only *partially* explain the differences in attitudes toward science across race/gender groups.

Table 11.2.　Descriptive Statistics, by Race and Gender Groups (General Social Survey 2008 and 2010)

	Full Sample (N = 2,006)	White Men (N = 761)	White Women (N = 133)	African American Men (N = 910)	African American Women (N = 202)
	Mean (SD)	Mean (SD)	Mean (SD)	Mean (SD)	Mean (SD)
Science does more harm than good (1 = strongly agree, 5 = strongly disagree)	3.700 (.021)	3.865 (.033)	3.733 (.030)**	3.308 (.094)***	3.168 (.072)***
Age (years)	48.804 (.376)	48.921 (.586)	50.645 (.577)*	44.526 (1.323)**	42.881 (1.134)***
Family income (2010 dollars)	27,111.42 (211.267)	28,794.35 (294.354)	27,214.84 (305.436)***	26,199.25 (904.549)***	20,905.94 (827.742)***
Education (years)	13.801 (.061)	13.963 (.102)	13.922 (.092)	12.970 (.222)***	13.193 (.164)***
Religiosity (1 = very religious, 4 = not religious)	2.417 (.022)	2.618 (.035)	2.349 (.032)***	2.293 (.083)***	2.050 (.062)***
Democrat (%)	36.042 (.011)	22.996 (.015)	34.176 (.015)***	67.669 (.041)***	72.772 (.031)***
Independent (%)	37.288 (.011)	44.021 (.018)	36.374 (.016)**	26.316 (.038)***	23.267 (.030)***
Republican (%)	26.670 (.013)	32.983 (.017)	29.451 (.015)	6.015 (.014)***	3.960 (.014)***

* .05 level, ** .005 level, *** .001 level

Table 11.3. Regression Predicting Attitudes toward "Modern Science Does More Harm Than Good," General Social Survey 2008 and 2010

	Model 1	Model 2
White women	−0.132**	−0.101*
African American men	−0.556***	−0.475***
African American women	−0.696***	−0.601***
Age		−0.0002
Income		0.001
Education		0.084***
Religiosity		0.135***
Democrat		0.117*
Independent		0.024
Constant	3.865***	2.283***

* .05 level, ** .005 level, *** .001 level
N = 2,006

Thus, in our quantitative analysis, we identified the broad trends in attitudes toward science by race and gender in the general public, noting that African American women have the most negative attitudes toward science out of the four race/gender groups we examined. We also confirmed some of the other key factors that shape people's attitudes toward science, as identified in previous research: education, religion, and politics. Still, questions remain about African American women's attitudes toward science. What knowledge and experiences are most salient as people consider whether science does more harm than good? What factors, in addition to those identified in the quantitative data, are relevant for understanding why people feel the way they do about science? These types of questions can best be answered with qualitative data. Thus, we will explore these questions in the following section, drawing on ten qualitative interviews with African American women.

QUALITATIVE FINDINGS

What Is Science?

In order to assess what our participants had in mind when responding to questions about "science," we analyzed responses to the broad questions about science, starting the interviews with the question: "Overall, modern science does more harm than good. Do you agree or disagree?" In their responses, participants talked about medicine, food,[3] technology, computers, and animals. Participants most commonly equated science with medicine. For example, Emery stated that some potential benefits of science could be "Getting to the root of some diseases we have. Just understanding the body. And what we're eating." Participants mentioned specific health and illness topics such as cancer; chemotherapy; stem cell research; vaccines for measles, mumps, and rubella; HIV; C-sections; ADD and ADHD; and depression. Participants also brought up other topics that were not related to medicine, including algorithms, automated assembly lines, caterpillars turning into butterflies, and testing laundry detergents for effectiveness. Some participants pushed back on questions about "science," suggesting that it was too broad a topic.

Benefits and Risks of Science

Participants largely disagreed with the statement "Overall, modern science does more harm than good" (McKenzie, Gloria, Emery, Caitlin, Brooklyn, Araminta, April). Two respondents agreed that science did more harm than good (London, Jet), and one participant did not understand the question (Autumn). When asked to elaborate on why she disagreed with the statement that modern science does more harm than good, McKenzie stated:

> I believe that modern science is essential in learning how to improve upon our world and where we live. And it's all through new medical developments that are developed through science. . . . I think the benefits are new cures that are found to treat HIV, cancer, and things like that. And from the medical perspective, I think that's very helpful. And I don't think we can have developed those things without modern sciences.

Given that the idea of "science" was often equated with medicine and many participants described the benefits of medical advances, it was not surprising that many participants held broadly favorable views on science. However, several participants held more unfavorable views about science as well as about medical research in particular. Some participants were deeply skeptical about scientists and scientific research, particularly as it related to health and illness. For example:

> Jet: Because they're doing things they shouldn't be doing. Making us more like guinea pigs, experimenting on us. They don't really know, they just kinda try it out. And if it doesn't work, they're like, "oh well we made a mistake."
>
> Joyce: In what ways do they experiment?
>
> Jet: Well, stem cells for one. They don't know what they're doing with that, and just experimenting to see if it works, you know. And not just that, our food too.

Other participants also commented broadly on systemic racism in medicine and medical research, as in the following two examples:

We've been in studies and we've been, we've been kinda the ones getting used. (Emery)

> I hold my race more important [than other identities] because I would say [that] the defining characteristic of myself is my race. And not so much that *I* view it that way as much as *others* view me that way. So it dictates how they deal with me. So it is the forefront of my mind. So in terms of racially, it dictates just like a certain level of distrust, you know, the Tuskegee experiments and whatnot. You just can't trust everybody, what they are shooting in your arms? They could say whatever they want to say that it is, but it doesn't mean anything. (Brooklyn)

While some participants explicitly related their mistrust in science to historical or contemporary racism in medicine, others also reported personal experiences with racism in seeking medical attention. As Emery stated,

> Because our eczema is different from white eczema, and I was prejudged even before being judged. So, I had little attitudes [from doctors] with that, like, "I can't help you." And I had a sour taste in my mouth from the white doctors. And then I met one . . . that kind of changed my perception. So, he was a rare one, but he was one.

Thus, our participants identified both the ways in which science has benefited humanity as a whole (specifically in terms of treating disease) but also the ways in which African Americans have been disproportionally harmed by science.

Explaining Views on Science: Lack of Knowledge, Exclusion, Political Views, and Religion

As noted earlier, the impact of a lack of knowledge about science has been a central focus of previous survey research on science attitudes. Many participants explicitly reflected on their lack of knowledge about science. This happened both in the context of broad questions about science and questions about science controversies. Participants' lack of knowledge was particularly evident when discussing science controversies. For example, when asked about her opinion on global warming, Gloria stated: "Now that's funny, I'm not sure. You know, I really haven't thought about it, to tell you the truth." Some participants had difficulty talking about science. For participants like Autumn, vague answers and misunderstanding of the questions can be attributed to her lack of experience with science; on the "science quiz," Autumn answered only one question correctly.

Some participants explicitly linked their lack of knowledge of science to their race, gender, and class identities. Of the three identities, narratives about race were the most common. For example, when asked about how being a woman of color and her social class shaped her attitudes toward global warming, McKenzie said, "Of course my race shapes how I think about it because I feel I'm not getting the option to know about it. And so I don't think as much as I should about it, and what I can do about it, because I just don't have the knowledge." In this response, McKenzie made an explicit connection between her lack of knowledge about science and her perceived exclusion from science.

Some participants traced their lack of knowledge about science to being discouraged from studying science in school. When asked about how being an African American woman and her social class shaped her views on science, Emery said,

Sometimes we feel like we're inadequate. . . . When we picked our classes, [they said] "Oh girl, you ain't gonna take that, that's hard." You always kinda had the negative of the science experience. . . . Sometimes we fall into that, which is bad. Everybody's crying about it, but ain't nobody trying to do nothing. And once you get in there [and study science], really it's not that bad.

Similarly, Araminta said,

I think being a woman period we don't really get taught science. Like it's not something that when I first started in school they encouraged. So, I kinda just didn't care about science. Although, I still kind of don't. [laughs] I don't *not* like it but it's just something that I don't find very interesting. But I feel like as a woman of color, I should be. I should be more into knowing what's happening with science now. All of the advancements in all the things that they're trying to do, I feel like I should know what's happening.

Notably, Araminta was one of two participants who earned a perfect score on the "science quiz," indicating that she has a high level of science literacy. However, Araminta still perceived a deficit in her ability to fully engage with science.

In addition to their personal experiences, participants described their broader perception that African Americans were excluded from science, given the lack of representation of African Americans in the scientific research community. For example, McKenzie stated, "from past experience, and my past knowledge about the field of science, there's not a lot of scientists that look like me, so how can it be for the overall good of everyone if I don't see none of my people there, or, if so, very few?"

Our quantitative analysis above demonstrated that political affiliations and religion are important predictors of attitudes toward science. Our interview participants had a strong connection to political party identities. Nine of ten

participants reported their political party affiliation as Democrat (one participant identified as an Independent with slightly liberal views). But participants
never explicitly discussed how their political beliefs shaped their views on
science. However, one participant alluded to the political implications of scientific knowledge. As April stated, "The harm, for me at least, is some of the
things we do with the information that we gather from science. The opinions
we create, the way we use science as a tool to make other opinions."

Participants were also homogeneous in their views on religion, as all identified as Christian. However, religion was rarely explicitly discussed. One
exception was Jet's response to a question about whether global warming was
due to human activity or natural causes:

> I believe it's a natural cause too. Because I know spiritually, the world is chang-
> ing things, and we're close to the end of times. It's the end times. It's supposed
> to do all this. What the Bible says is gonna happen is happening. People just
> don't want to believe that's what it is, so they make themselves feel better and
> not be afraid. They say it's caused by gases or whatever. I'm sure that doesn't
> help the atmosphere, I'm pretty sure it doesn't. But I don't think that's the main
> problem with what's going on.

At first glance, the fact that religious and political attitudes strongly impacted
views on science in the quantitative analysis but discussion of religion and
politics did not frequently appear in the interview data might suggest that
these two sources of data are providing contradictory findings. However,
we argue that they are entirely consistent, given our conceptualization of
a cognitive aspect of public perception. In our interpretation, our interview
participants, who held fairly strong political and religious views, have drawn
on these modes of knowledge to develop general dispositions toward science.
These general dispositions shape how participants talk about science, rather
than being explicitly articulated by participants.

DISCUSSION

In this project, we integrated quantitative and qualitative analysis to provide
a fuller picture of African American women's views on science. The mixed-
methods approach allowed us to utilize the benefits of both approaches. The
survey data demonstrated the broad trends in the public while the interviews
offered an in-depth understanding at one particular intersection of race and
gender. If we looked only at the quantitative data, we would miss the impact
of discrimination and exclusion. If we looked only at the qualitative data,
we would miss the importance of political and religious views as underly-

ing dispositions. In combination, we gain a better understanding of African American women's attitudes toward science.

In the final analysis, we argue that African American women's more negative attitudes toward science are a result of a complex history of oppression and their unique intersection of race and gender. Our findings, taken together with previous research, indicate that African American women's beliefs about the harms of science should be understood within the context of experiences with race- and gender-based discrimination and exclusion (e.g., medical professionals, schools), underrepresentation in science (e.g., lack of African American women scientists), and the historical and ongoing harm that medical science has inflicted on African American communities. This research indicates that studies focused on people's attitudes and perceptions about science should consider how intersecting identities influence people's inclusion and engagement with science as well as trust in science, including the institutions that disseminate science knowledge.

NOTES

1. We also asked participants about their political views on a seven-point scale of very liberal to very conservative. However, some participants were not familiar with the labels of liberal, moderate, and conservative and opted to skip this question.

2. Several participants rejected the idea that their race or gender shaped their attitudes toward science broadly (Autumn, Caitlin, Gloria) and several additional participants rejected the idea that their race or gender shaped their views on specific topics.

3. At the time of the interviews, there was a ballot initiative in Oregon about labeling genetically modified foods; several participants brought up the topics of food and genetically modified foods.

REFERENCES

Bauer, Martin W., Nick Allum, and Steve Miller. 2007. "What Can We Learn from 25 Years of PUS Survey Research? Liberating and Expanding the Agenda." *Public Understanding of Science* 16(1): 79–95.

DiMaggio, Paul. 1997. "Culture and Cognition." *Annual Review of Sociology* 23(1): 263–87.

Elder, Laurel, Steven Greene, and Mary Kate Lizotte. 2018. "The Gender Gap on Public Opinion towards Genetically Modified Foods." *Social Science Journal* 55(4): 500–509.

Gauchat, Gordon W. 2011. "The Cultural Authority of Science: Public Trust and Acceptance of Organized Science." *Public Understanding of Science* 20(6): 751–70.

————. 2012. "Politicization of Science in the Public Sphere: A Study of Public Trust in the United States, 1974 to 2010." *American Sociological Review* 77(2): 167–87.

Gauchat, Gordon W., and Kenneth T. Andrews. 2018. "The Cultural-Cognitive Mapping of Scientific Professions." *American Sociological Review* 83(3): 567–95.

Hanson, S. 2009. *Swimming against the Tide: African American Girls and Science Education*. Philadelphia: Temple University Press.

Hayes, Bernadette C., and Vicki N. Tariq. 2000. "Gender Differences in Scientific Knowledge and Attitudes toward Science: A Comparative Study of Four Anglo-American Nations." *Public Understanding of Science* 9(4): 433–47.

Miller, Jon D. 2004. "Public Understanding of, and Attitudes toward, Scientific Research: What We Know and What We Need to Know." *Public Understanding of Science* 13(3): 273–94.

Morgan, David L. 2014. *Integrating Qualitative and Quantitative Methods: A Pragmatic Approach*. Thousand Oaks, CA: Sage.

Perry, B., T. Link, C. Boelter, and C. Leukefeld. 2012. "Blinded to Science: Gender Differences in the Effects of Race, Ethnicity, and Socioeconomic Status on Academic and Science Attitudes among Sixth Graders." *Gender and Education* 24(7): 725–43.

Plutzer, Eric. 2013. "The Racial Gap in Confidence in Science: Explanations and Implications." *Bulletin of Science, Technology & Society* 33(5–6): 146–57.

Scharff, Darcell P., Katherine J. Mathews, Pamela Jackson, Jonathan Hoffsuemmer, Emeobong Martin, and Dorothy Edwards. 2010. "More Than Tuskegee: Understanding Mistrust about Research Participation." *Journal of Health Care for the Poor and Underserved* 21(3): 879–97.

Sturgis, P., and N. Allum. 2001. "Gender Differences in Scientific Knowledge and Attitudes toward Science: Reply to Hayes and Tariq." *Public Understanding of Science* 10(4): 427–30.

Vaisey, Stephen. 2009. "Motivation and Justification: A Dual-Process Model of Culture in Action." *American Journal of Sociology* 114(6):1675–1715.

Westergaard, Ryan P., Mary Catherine Beach, Somnath Saha, and Elizabeth A. Jacobs. 2014. "Racial/Ethnic Differences in Trust in Health Care: HIV Conspiracy Beliefs and Vaccine Research Participation." *Journal of General Internal Medicine* 29(1): 140–46.

Chapter 12

Doing Intersectional Mixed-Methods Feminist Research

Maura Kelly and Joyce McNair

MAURA'S REFLECTION

The idea for the project on African American women and science started with Gordon Gauchat's quantitative research on attitudes toward science. He observed that the research in this area rarely took intersectional or mixed-methods approaches; he wanted to do both. He first recruited two friends and colleagues from graduate school: Katie Acosta (an expert on race, gender, and qualitative research) and me (an expert on gender and mixed-methods research). My Portland State University graduate student research assistants also contributed to this project: PhD candidate Elizabeth Withers conducted the quantitative analyses that appear in our empirical chapter and assisted with writing the quantitative portion of the methods section and master's candidate Joyce McNair conducted the qualitative interviews and assisted with writing the qualitative portion of the methods section. As a team, we worked through a variety of issues related to doing this research in line with key elements of feminist methodology.

In this chapter, I first describe some of the behind-the-scenes decisions that went into the research design: developing the interview guide, recruitment, compensation, determining where to interview participants, and race and gender matching of interviewer and participants. Then Joyce reflects on her experiences as the interviewer for this project and how her positionality as an African American woman impacted this research.

Developing the interview guide for the qualitative component of this project was a very interesting experience because this topic was pretty different from my previous research. In most of my research, I have asked participants to tell me about the things that happen in their daily lives, mostly about their jobs. In this project, we asked participants to talk about science, something many people don't talk or think about on a regular basis. We put a lot of work into refining the questions on the interview guide. For example, in the first draft of the interview guide, the very first question was "What is science?" I initially thought this was a great question! It would allow us to know what immediately came to participants' minds when first presented with the concept of "science." When we began testing out the interview guide in pilot interviews (practice interviews not included in the final sample), we found out that this question was terrible. Those early volunteer participants (family and friends of my graduate student research assistants) didn't know how to answer the question and became uncomfortable or embarrassed. So that question had to go. Another decision we made was about how to ask our participants about intersectional identities. We wanted to ask about race, gender, and class, so we could have asked a series of questions such as "How does your *race* shape how you think about science? How does your *gender*? How does your *class*?" But we did not want to insist that our participants artificially separate these identities. So we asked, "How does *being a woman of color and your class* shape how you think about science?" This gave our participants opportunity to reflect on any or all of these identities in their responses to this question. This question was not always easy for participants to answer, but we wanted to explicitly ask participants to reflect on how their multiple identities were salient in their views on science, in addition to noting where discussions of gender, race, and class came up spontaneously in the participants' responses.

For this project, we only had funding and time for a small qualitative study of ten participants, so we knew we would need to have a purposive, rather than a random, sample. To recruit our participants, we decided to focus on two historically African American neighborhoods in North Portland. I'm fortunate that my wife is a graphic designer who is willing to create recruitment flyers for my research projects (see figure 12.1). We put our flyers up in two library branches, the local branch of Portland Community College (PCC), and a variety of businesses. Joyce made a connection with a staff member of the women's center at PCC, who referred several participants for the study. We also used snowball sampling, in which a participant refers additional participants for the project. This can be an effective method for recruiting participants who might be mistrustful of research. A potential participant is likely to trust a friend or family member who recommends participating in research after having a positive experience.

For this study, we felt it was important to offer compensation for participation. Our participants were sharing their valuable time and knowledge and we wanted to give them something in exchange. A second practical reason for this compensation was that it is much easier to recruit people if you have

Figure 12.1. Recruitment flyer for science attitudes study by Kendra Kelly of Coffee Rings Design

something to offer them rather than just asking for volunteers. Ultimately, we offered each participant $20 as compensation for a one-hour interview. As Joyce notes in her reflection below, this money was meaningful to participants; not necessarily just because of what it could buy, but because it showed that we valued their knowledge and time.

We wanted our participants to feel comfortable at the interviews, so we decided not to have our participants come to the Portland State University campus. We knew our participants might potentially have negative perceptions of research and a university campus can be intimidating; we preferred to conduct the interviews in more familiar settings. Further, the Portland State campus is located downtown, and would not be convenient for many participants living in North Portland. Instead, we looked into reserving private study rooms in libraries in the neighborhood where we recruited participants. Ultimately, interviews were conducted in the library of the community college located in the neighborhood. A few participants attended school on this campus, and for the others it was a short walk, drive, or public transit ride from home.

From early on in the development of the project, we felt that it was important to race and gender match our interviewer and participants. Race and gender matching can be a way to make participants feel more comfortable in the interview, particularly when the interview includes topics related to race and gender identities. Race and gender matching are not always necessary; it depends on the project and the logistical issues of having available interviewers of the same race and gender as the participants. Drawing on feminist methodology, it is critical that researchers be reflexive about both shared and different identities, and how these might matter for data collection. For this project, I was lucky that Joyce, an African American woman graduate student, had recently come to my office to ask if I had any research projects she might join. As a more experienced researcher who usually does most of the interviews for the qualitative projects I work on, it was a little challenging for me to turn the reins over to Joyce. And when I read the transcripts, there were places where I would have asked a question differently or maybe probed a little further to get more information. But there were also follow-up questions that Joyce posed that I wouldn't have thought to ask. And most importantly, our participants spoke freely about their experiences of racism and sexism, which was facilitated by the shared identities between researcher and participant. Ultimately, the interviews for this project had very rich information and I know that Joyce was a better person for this job.

JOYCE'S REFLECTION

As a first-year graduate student, it was music to my ears when I was given an opportunity to participate in a research project that would list my name as an author in a published work. When I discovered that the research was designed to gain the opinions of African American women's views and exposure to science, I was delighted. As an African American woman, I am interested in how African American women view the intersection of gender, race, and science. I helped to edit the interview guide to ensure that potential participants would not feel uncomfortable when asked the questions. I also ensured that these edits did not compromise the integrity of the study.

Interviewing African American women was empowering for me. Upon entering the interview room, participants smiled when they saw that I was an African American woman as well. During the interview, I assured participants that they could decline any questions and speak freely in an environment where they would not be judged for their responses or their lack of knowledge regarding the subject matter. I believe that that added to the depth and complexity in participant responses.

In the interviews, participants appeared relaxed and at ease. This was noticeable in their body language and facial expressions. Several participants commented on my achievement as an interviewer; two participants hugged me; and three gave me high-fives, signifying their support of my position and achievement.

The most exciting experience of interviewing was at the end of the interviews. Participants smiled and thanked me for two reasons: someone cared enough to ask them their opinions and was willing to compensate them for their time and any inconvenience.

Chapter 13

Not Your Indian

The Meanings of Indigenous Identity at Standing Rock

Barbara Gurr

In June 2016 Energy Transfer Partners (ETP), a US-based natural gas and propane company, began construction on an oil pipeline that would eventually cross fifty counties and four states. Thousands of people from across the Americas and from around the world traveled to Standing Rock Reservation in North Dakota between April 2016 and February 2017 to oppose the construction of the Dakota Access pipeline and its proposed route across the Missouri River, five miles from the federally recognized reservation boundary. I joined the water protectors (their preferred term) at Standing Rock twice and witnessed the growth of the gathering there as it became the largest environmental protest in US history[1] and the most diverse gathering of indigenous peoples the world has seen in recorded history.

Although environmental sustainability was perhaps the most publicly visible theme of the multiple camps that gathered at Standing Rock, there was in fact far more at stake, and far more being claimed; events at Standing Rock also highlighted the dynamic complexities of indigenous identity and endurance, marked by discourses that simultaneously competed, elided, and coordinated with each other. Individual and collective identities form through a variety of dialectical and dynamic means (Aroopala 2012; Hecht 1993), including interactions between personal and social identities and interactions between groups (Tajfel 2010; Turner and Tajfel 1986). Standing Rock provided a crucible in which identity, already fraught for Native Americans with multiple and often competing understandings, was alternately acknowledged, validated, and erased.

In this chapter, I focus on assertions of indigeneity that emerged and coalesced at Standing Rock by considering some of the events and interactions that reflected and reified certain identity discourses; how these events may have been understood by different actors; and how those ways of understanding identity were built, sustained, disseminated, and received. These various understandings of what it means to be indigenous reveal the deeply political nature of indigenous identity following over five centuries of settler colonialism. Identity claims of indigenous people at Standing Rock reflect current and historical denial of indigenous specificity, and are thus reflective of the constraints imposed by dominant, white supremacist culture, but also reveal the work of self-creation and self-maintenance outside of dominant frames as the claim to a historical, continuous existence and way of life that predates settler colonialism and potentially reveals a resistance rooted in identity that is not entirely predetermined by other circulating meanings about indigeneity.

Materialist feminist approaches often consider discourse from Foucauldian perspectives that attempt to recognize the production of meaning through multiple, interacting discursive artifacts, for example, mainstream news and social media (e.g., Hennessy 1993; Naples 2002, 2003), but here there is a potentially overdetermined assumption of constraint on social movement actors, as many scholars argue that identity frames are shaped by existing discourses and power relations. However, claims made by Native people themselves about the meaning of indigeneity, although often in response to dominant social and political discourses about identity, also clearly reflect an agency rooted in historical context and shaped by an enduring sense of belonging to a specific geography. In this way, indigenous identity supersedes contemporary or historical meanings produced by non-indigenous actors, but simultaneously responds to these same external impositions, reflecting the complexity of indigenous identity in what is now called the United States.

DATA AND METHODS

My larger project considering events at Standing Rock utilizes a wide methodological net to better understand the complex nexus of identity claims made at Standing Rock: critical discourse analysis, participant observation, interviews, critical and iconographic analysis of protest art and music, and archival research, all collected and conducted between August 2016 and August 2017.

Twelve in-depth interviews with water protectors who self-identified as indigenous were conducted at Standing Rock and associated events, as well as innumerable informal conversations with both Native and non-Native actors at Standing Rock and other locations. For example, I conducted interviews in Washington, DC, immediately following the Native Nations March in March 2017 and on the campus of a large research university with a Native American student who had both been to Standing Rock and helped organize a rally on

her campus in support of the water protectors. While most interview participants were found through snowball sampling beginning with people I already
knew, several were completely serendipitous, such as my interview with a
woman who worked at a convenience store on Standing Rock Reservation.
This convenience store happened to be close to the resistance camps and was
frequented by water protectors looking for gas, water, and similar items. I was
a regular customer there on both of my trips, picking up energy drinks for the
guards at the camp and coffee for myself, and Estelle and I got to know each
other casually before I asked her for an interview. She then introduced me to
her brother Beau, who also gave me an interview.

However, as fruitful as interviews were, participant observation as I visited
Standing Rock in October and November 2016 and attended numerous actions there and elsewhere between October 2016 and April 2017 proved even
more so. Marches, rallies, and other events offered the opportunity to observe
visual representations of indigeneity ranging from personal embodiment
(hairstyle and length, clothing, tattoos) to posters, banners, and other artwork,
and also observe music, language, and even food and semi-permanent dwellings. Similarly, informal conversations offered opportunities to elaborate on
collective meanings in ways that formal interviews often missed.

In the year following my two visits to Standing Rock, I also conducted
a wide-ranging critical discourse analysis, an approach that examines how
power relations potentially impact how we think about people and social
organization, to better understand the multiple ways events at Standing Rock
were understood, the identity claims that shaped those events, and how each
was produced and disseminated. Because access to certain forms of public
discourse is not evenly distributed or utilized across different populations, I
conceptualized discourse broadly. For example, law enforcement may have
different access to public media than grassroots water protectors; different
groups may also choose different forms of communication, such as mainstream news or social media. I collected and analyzed news clips, articles, blog
posts, YouTube videos, Facebook posts, and public statements from political
and oil industry leaders as well as water protectors and indigenous leaders, but
also considered numerous iconographic artifacts such as posters and banners,
as well as the music that was played at certain events and written about Standing Rock. The archive of this material consists of close to 150 items ranging
from mainstream news pieces (such as CNN or Reuters) to Facebook posts
and videos from the protectors, graffiti art, music, and music videos.

I coded each of these for common themes and dialogic interactions; amount
of time or space given to different parties (such as county police, water protectors, and local citizens); visual representation (for example, Native people
in public protests who wore tradition-oriented clothes and law enforcement

in uniform as well as what type of uniform, for example, street uniforms or SWAT uniforms); and even, when possible, number of views or likely readership (for example, noting "likes" and other comments on Facebook, number of views and comments on YouTube, and subscription readership).

For this chapter, I utilize data from interviews, participant observation, and discourse analysis to consider three intersecting understandings of indigeneity and the ways in which these understandings are produced and enacted. I rely on a partially auto-ethnographic lens to highlight not only the discourses around me but also my own experiences of these discourses, thereby including myself as a source of data, as well. Auto-ethnography, in which the researcher writes with obvious intent her own presence into the analysis, potentially produces a democratic space of knowledge production, rather than a seemingly (but never really) unbiased "expert" performance of knowledge for others to simply consume. In this chapter, I use auto-ethnography to contextualize my analysis and provide the reader with as full a picture as possible of the experiences that helped drive this analysis.

"THOSE PEOPLE": THE MEANING OF INDIGENEITY OFF THE REZ

I first traveled to Standing Rock for Indigenous Day weekend in October 2016. A website maintained by one of the camps at Standing Rock warned of a roadblock on the drive from Bismarck to the reservation, but I was surprised by its size—several police vehicles as well as an armored car, with several Morton County police officers and members of the National Guard milling about. The roadblock had gone up shortly after a violent altercation between water protectors and private security hired by ETP during which security dogs attacked water protectors, and the extent of the roadblock intended to prevent, or at least screen, access to the reservation indicated a general mistrust of travelers to and from the reservation. When a National Guardsman stopped my car and asked me where I was going, I was very aware of the fraught politics of the time and place (and the uniformed weapons surrounding me); I lied and told him I was trying to get to Sioux Falls, several hours past Standing Rock.

"Well, you can't go down this road because of the trouble with those people down there," he replied. I looked at him blankly. "Down on that reservation," he added helpfully.

"Is everything all right down there?" I asked him.

"Just fine," he replied. "But there are some protesters and they've been getting aggressive. If you take this route you can avoid the mess," he added, handing me a map and showing me the alternate route—an unpaved road for several more miles that would eventually loop around so I could enter the reservation from the south.

I thanked him, took the turn indicated, and then stopped to take a picture of the roadblock. However, when I stood from my car with my camera, several police and guardsmen walked toward me waving their arms and telling me, "No pictures, no pictures." Although the authorities at the roadblock were clearly surveilling all who passed, they prohibited return surveillance, exerting control over the visual narrative that could emerge from their actions.

This is the discourse about Standing Rock that existed, and flourished, off the reservation. Indeed, for anyone traveling from the nearest airport and the nearest large city this frame served as a literal gateway to be navigated in order to enter "that reservation," or better yet, to heed the indirect warning and avoid "the mess" created by "those people down there," and the more direct warning that they were "getting aggressive." This is how one side told and controlled the story of Standing Rock: implying violence and danger among presumably lawless Natives while limiting alternative narratives. It was a description that was picked up over and over throughout North Dakota media that fall, for example, by KFYR TV, the local Fox news affiliate, which published a piece titled "Reporters threatened at DAPL protest camp" in October 2016; the first line proclaims, "More violent behavior from Dakota Access Pipeline protesters is causing great concern among Morton County authorities." The piece continues, "Officers say the situation escalated into a very threatening and terrifying experience" and quotes the reporters, who did not specify any threats made against them, saying, "we're in danger and we're surrounded" (Berlinger 2016). It is not until the very end of the piece that the reporters' lack of press credentials and refusal to identify which news agency they worked for is briefly mentioned, nor were these two potentially pertinent facts pursued in subsequent reporting that might have revealed more about the reporters themselves: their role at the camps, for example, and whether they were legitimate press. This narrative of DAPL "protesters" threatening innocent people who then needed protection from law enforcement was encouraged and elaborated upon by the Morton County Sheriff's Department as well as elected North Dakota officials, the upper management of ETP, and everyday North Dakotans who hoped the pipeline would bring jobs to their state.

For example, a month after this trip, Reuters reported that North Dakota's Governor Dalrymple proposed a blockade less than a mile from the camps for the purpose of preventing supplies from reaching the protectors; his office explained that this was in the interest of "public safety" (Sylvester 2016). This occurred shortly after the Morton County Sheriff's office

Photo 13.1. The blockade closing down highway 1806, less than a mile from *Oceti Sakowin* camp

defended increased aggression against protectors because "this is a public safety issue. . . . We cannot have protesters blocking county roads, block- ing state highways, or trespassing on private property" (Silva 2016). The blockade was instituted on Highway 1806 less than a mile from the camps, and completely blocked access to the camps and the reservation from that direction, limiting the movements not only of protectors, but also of emer- gency vehicles and residents of the reservation (see photo 13.1), a decision with dangerous consequences just a couple of weeks later when violence erupted between police and protectors. In this scenario, it was clear that the "public" being kept safe did not include Native citizens.

Local media aided in the production of this narrative of dangerous Native Americans who needed to be contained by roadblocks and aggressive action to protect the safety of the general population by State actors (the governor's office, the local police, and the National Guard). The *Bismarck Tribune*, the second-largest newspaper in North Dakota with a readership of over 25,000, proclaimed in an editorial that "The *Tribune* has been supportive of pipelines as a means of moving oil since the oil boom began" (McCleary 2016a), and its support of the Dakota Access Pipeline had been clear and consistent throughout the months of encampment at Standing Rock; the paper consis- tently espoused an analysis of events that generally favored the oil company and local police. Although Tribal leaders were often interviewed, interviews with state and local, non-Tribal authorities were given more coverage and protectors were rarely interviewed at all. Similarly, the paper's consistent use of the words "protesters" and "protests" to describe the people and events on and around Standing Rock was in direct opposition to protectors' insistence that they were not protesting the pipeline, but rather, protecting the water (this protection was later explicitly extended to the land and treaty rights, as in the formation of a third camp called the "1851 Treaty Camp," but water remained the primary focus). Additionally, opinion pieces published by the paper regularly described Native protectors and their allies in negative terms, such as the opinion piece written by Ron Ness (2016), president of the North Dakota Petroleum Association, who opened his piece by describing the water protectors as "lawless," "intimidating," and "terrorist."

At times this discourse of indigenous actors as dangerous was tempered to a simple dismissal of indigeneity as a distinct identity claim, as on my second trip to Standing Rock. I had dressed hastily for my early morning flight for this trip, throwing on a sweatshirt that proclaimed "It's all Indian Land" across the back. While I would like to say that wearing this sweatshirt was part of an activist ethos, I had actually given it no thought whatsoever—it was just close at hand when I dressed in the predawn darkness. I gave it no thought at all, in fact, until I landed in Bismarck and stood in line at the rental car agency in front of two men dressed for hunting and carrying gun cases. One of the men said to me, "This ain't no Indian land anymore, sweetheart. This is just America now." I explained briefly that numerous treaties in fact legally set aside certain tracts of land solely for Native people, but the man shook his head. "Those treaties were a long time ago," he informed me. Then he asked, "Is this about that oil pipeline?" I nodded. "I don't know why they gotta make such a fuss over that," he said. "They use oil, don't they? Everybody uses oil. We need it." His friend nodded in agreement.

Setting aside their claim that our reliance on oil is inevitable (and the patronizing, sexist way in which he made this claim) and the casual laying of blame on Native people who "make such a fuss," this brief conversation reveals a very specific claim about indigeneity: "this is just America now" whitewashes the presence of Native people, subsuming them into a melting pot that denies cultural and historical specificity, and certainly rejects the validity of ongoing claims by Native people to land and water rights. For this non-Native man, there is no unique claim to indigeneity—this is all just America now. We all use oil. We are all the same. *Not* indigenous, or perhaps *all* indigenous; *E pluribus unum*, "out of the many one." If we are all "one," then claims to a specific (and preexisting) identity are null.

As well as describing Native actors as "terrorists" or claims to Indian land as no longer relevant, a third understanding began to emerge in the closing months of events at Standing Rock, one in which the tribe and its claims to sovereignty were recognized but this recognition was used to call for the tribe's greater investment in mainstream approaches. In an editorial at the end of December 2016, the *Tribune* noted that "it's not unreasonable for the tribe to want to control their destiny on the reservation. It's understandable they want to be consulted about projects close to their borders and projects that could impact their water supply" (McCleary 2016b). This statement marked a shift in the paper's general reporting and was printed three weeks after hundreds of US veterans arrived at Standing Rock to protect the protectors from increasing police violence. However, the same editorial notes that "The Standing Rock Sioux Tribe appears to be moving in the right direction as it considers a tribal utilities commission" and that the commission "could help avoid situations like the Dakota Access Pipeline" (McCleary 2016b). Virtually no mention was made of the role of ETP, the police, or private security hired by ETP in the tensions around Standing Rock and the Dakota Access Pipeline; nor does the editorial mention the local government's focus on keeping only certain citizens "safe," or the failure of the Environmental Protection Agency to properly consult with the tribe. Instead, responsibility was placed solely with the tribe for both cause and solution, a common theme in North Dakota news coverage and in my own conversations with North Dakota citizens not involved in the actions at Standing Rock.

Off the reservation (the "rez"), "those people down there" were variously understood as a public menace that must be contained, as essentially nonexistent as a distinct People, and as reasonable citizens who had simply failed in their prescribed civic role but were now complying with expectations. These meanings reflect broader historical erasure of Native people from public discourse as well as ongoing political erasure of their sovereignty and cultural distinctiveness. While these discourses dominated mainstream news coverage and non-Native people's understandings of the Native people at Standing Rock, I found a variety of counter-discourses about Native identity being produced by water protectors at Standing Rock.

"OUR LAND": INDIGENOUS IDENTITY AT STANDING ROCK

My drive through Standing Rock Reservation on my first trip was peaceful; the wide-open land was still surprisingly green in early October, dotted with free-running horses and the occasional glimpse of the fabled, now contentious, Missouri River in the distance. I knew I had reached *Oceti Sakowin* (Lakota for "seven council fires") camp when I glimpsed several tipis over a small hill. Turning right to enter the camp, I stopped at a makeshift guard shack to introduce myself to Mel, who I found out was a Gulf War veteran and member of the American Indian Movement (AIM). There were several veterans and AIM members volunteering their time as *akicita*, guardians of the camp whose job was to ensure that everyone behaved appropriately. "No drugs," I told him, already knowing the rules, which were also posted at the entrance. "No alcohol. I've got my camera, but I don't really know how to use it, and I won't take any pictures without permission."

"Weapons?"

"No way," I said emphatically. "I didn't even bring nail clippers."

Mel laughed and glanced around the inside of my car. "Where you from?"

"Connecticut."

"Connecticut!" Mel whistled, leaning his arm, tattooed with an eagle feather, against my car door. "That's a long way! What brings you out here?"

"I came to stand with you all," I told him seriously, feeling a little shy.

"Well, thank you for coming!" He grinned. "*Wopila!*" (the Lakota word for an especially important kind of gratitude, as opposed to *pilamaya*, similar to the more casual "thanks"). "Welcome to *Oceti Sakowin.* Do you know where you're going?"

I glanced down the long Avenue of Flags, a well-worn dirt road bordered on both sides with flags from the numerous indigenous nations from around the world that had already come to Standing Rock to show their support. "Not really," I admitted. "I'm looking for a friend, though." I told him my friend's name and Mel brightened further.

"Oh, sure, you'll find her around somewhere," he assured me. He gave me directions to the cook tent and the portable toilets, then suggested a place to park while I searched for my friend. "You let me know if you need anything!" he shouted after me as I pulled away.

This version of Standing Rock was certainly different from what the National Guardsman had implied. But it, too, was a gateway—I had to be checked out and declared safe before I could enter *Oceti Sakowin* camp. I had to know the rules—no drugs, no alcohol, no weapons. Just as importantly, I knew someone whom Mel knew, and being able to drop her name, unintentional as it was, offered an assurance to Mel that I was a legitimate ally. This was more important than I realized at the time; private security groups and possibly the federal government had already begun to infiltrate the camps and report back to ETP, as well as allegedly local and state police and possibly the FBI (e.g., Barat 2017; Democracy Now 2017a, 2017b).

I drove slowly down the Avenue of Flags, trying to read each one and also watching out for children and dogs (there were several of each darting across the road). After I parked I strolled through the camp, my camera draped around my neck backward, with the lens cap on (taking pictures without permission is rude anywhere, but particularly in Native space. I didn't want to make anyone uncomfortable). There was a small Two Spirit encampment, covered in rainbows, with a friendly sign welcoming visitors. On the other hand, at the far edge of the camp was the Red Warrior encampment, a small group of tipis with a large rope looped around them and a sign warning that not only were visitors *not* welcome, neither were cameras. I, a white woman visiting with a camera, scurried by as quickly as possible.

On my first trip to Standing Rock, I was struck by the ever-presence of indigeneity. Several indigenous languages were spoken, although Lakota dominated, and directional signs were as often written in Lakota as in English. AIM flags could be seen throughout the camp, and of course the Avenue of Flags proudly and visibly displayed the breadth of not only national but global indigenous support for the protectors. Tipis were everywhere, and the sounds of drumming and singing could be heard all around the camp.

The elders of the Lakota Nation remained adamant throughout the months of the camp's existence that the gathering at Standing Rock was a ceremony, meaning that while we were there, we were to remain prayerful and behave in tradition-oriented ways. This meant that there was a certain level of gender segregation, women predominantly performing certain chores and occupying certain spaces and men others, although there was unavoidable mingling at all times; it was a camp, after all, and resources were shared widely. Most people dressed modestly—women (including me) wore long skirts over their jeans and men also stayed fully covered. People were expected to treat each other respectfully and be helpful to the camp overall. There were prayer ceremonies held throughout the day, and the main circle in *Oceti Sakowin* camp, a place to socialize, gather information, and welcome new protectors, also held a sacred fire that was kept burning throughout the duration of the camp's existence.

These ubiquitous enactments of tradition-oriented Lakota behavior served to remind protectors at the camps, both Native and non-Native, that this was indigenous land and an indigenous-led movement. Although *akicita* were present throughout the camps for security, for the most part, expectations were simply expressed so thoroughly and in so many ways, and were enacted so publicly, that behaving in contradiction to these expectations became harder than simply meeting them, and certainly more noticeable. The ability of the community to police itself without formal enforcement structures was, itself, an expression of tradition-oriented behavior reflective of historical practice. It is a kind of social control that differs somewhat from mainstream society's; visitors were expected to figure out the right way to behave for the good of the collective by following the social cues of others, and then to behave that way.

On my second trip out to Standing Rock I found that *Oceti Sakowin* camp had grown to almost 7,000 people. This trip was at the end of November, immediately following the events of Sunday, November 20, when Morton County Police doused protectors with water cannons in sub-zero temperatures and a young woman's arm was nearly blown off, allegedly by a concussion grenade thrown by a police officer (evidence was confiscated by the Morton County Police and the FBI and has yet to be returned to the young woman's lawyer as of this writing). The mainstream media paid attention to those events and the general reporting that followed largely presented that night as one of brutal State tactics against unarmed underdogs. Allies flocked to the reservation. Many of these were college students on Thanksgiving break, and many were adults who had left home and family to be a part of the movement to protect the Missouri River.

The constant reminders of whose land we were on, of the insistent existence of indigeneity, had multiplied by my second trip, but there were competing changes, as well; thousands more non-Natives had joined the camps, bringing different kinds of music, different kinds of dwellings, and even different smells as individual cooking fires overwhelmed the burning of sage and sweetgrass. With more people came more trash and more portable bathrooms throughout the camps, as well as more vehicles. More than once I overheard reminders that "it's not a festival"—the protectors were here to do the hard work of protecting the water, land, and treaty rights, not to dance in the roadways to Phish and the Grateful Dead. In some ways, then, although the presence of indigeneity still filled the senses there was a strong overlay of settler presence that both wove throughout the camps and even occasionally overwhelmed the indigeneity it was purportedly there to support. Many of my informants expressed concern that Standing Rock's leap into a kind of cause célèbre also potentially produced a loss of control for indigenous leaders, who maintained that the original rules—no drugs, no alcohol, no weapons—continue to be followed, but the Elders' Council insisted that all who were there to protect the water were welcome.

However, despite the success of informal social policing, things didn't always go smoothly. The camps were open to all who came, and the diversity of protectors produced a diversity of behaviors. More often than not it seemed from both my own observations and stories I heard from others, to be instances of racial privilege that unintentionally set non-Natives apart from Natives. On my first trip to the camp, a white family arrived late in the evening and set up their pop-up camper in the middle of a roadway, blocking other cars from entering or exiting the area easily. Granted, it was a dirt roadway and it was getting dark when they arrived, so the next morning, assuming they hadn't realized their mistake, an elder approached them and asked them to move their camp so others could use the roadway. They didn't, and their camper's location forced all of us to drive around them through a much bumpier area. The elder, a woman who has both been involved in AIM and was a founding member of Women of All Red Nations, spoke angrily and with disappointment about "people who don't even know any better, even though I told 'em! That is white privilege! This is *our* land," she told me. "They're guests here!"[2]

It was an assertion of belonging, and who does not belong, that was echoed numerous times in multiple ways during both of my stays at the camp, including in my interview with a Lakota elder who had been at *Oceti Sakowin* since its formation. I asked Bernice what she thought of the Army Corps of Engineers' letter to the tribe, sent in early December, asking that the camps be disbanded. She replied, "Yeah, they've tried that before. They're always asking us to move, to leave. We're not going anywhere." I asked her what she thought of all the people gathered at the camps—thousands at that point, many of them non-Native—and she replied, "Lakota people have always been here. You white people are new to this land, and I guess it's great that some of you want to be here and help out. But we've always been here. This is *our* land. We belong here." Bernice's assertion that white people are "new to this land," despite five hundred years of occupation, reflects a sense of belonging that is deeply rooted in a long, enduring history. This sense of who belongs to the land, and particularly that specific geographic area, and who does not was expressed in other interviews and conversations, such as a brief exchange I had with Jenny, a white woman with whom I washed dishes in the cook tent, who explained, "We're all just visitors here, honey. You and I are guests."

All three of these women expressed an understanding of indigeneity that reflected a profound historical relationship with *that* land. Who "belonged" *there* and who was a "guest" was determined by the Lakota people collectively, not the protectors individually, the Army Corps of Engineers, or the visitors themselves. This assertion of belonging *there*, to *that* land, was further reflected in the name of the third camp, the 1851 Treaty Camp, a small camp created for the express purpose of guarding a small tract of land and named after a treaty between the Lakota Nation and the United States.

GENDER AND RACE AT *OCETI SAKOWIN*

During my second visit I joined a women's prayer walk (see photo 13.2). It was made clear to us at the start that the purpose was to amplify Native women's voices, though all women were welcome to join. Men were not, and were asked to stay back once we reached the barricaded bridge blocking route 1806. The only men to move forward with us were *akicita*, and they remained silent and out of our way—they were there only for protection.

At one point as we stood facing the armed police and their armored tanks, several women began to sing a prayer song in Lakota. A white woman standing next to me, not knowing the words, began to sing the Christian hymn "Amazing Grace" and was joined by several other white women. I stood between these white women and several Native women, hearing the Lakota prayer song on one side and the Christian hymn sung in English on the other, and wondered about the sense of privilege—whether racial, religious, linguistic, or some other flavor—that led the white women to overlay the Lakota prayer song with their own assertion of faith, rather than simply offer the silent support of their presence. I assume that these women, whom I didn't have an opportunity to ask, wanted to offer their support in an active, vocal way, but having been told in no uncertain terms that this walk, organized and led by Native women, was intended to centralize Native women's voices, it is hard to imagine this as anything other than an ignorant inability on the parts of these white women to remain silent and allow Native women to be heard clearly. This, too, reflects an understanding about indigeneity—one perhaps emerging from a desire for solidarity as women, but reflecting a chasm of racial and cultural difference as these white women were somehow able to ignore the specific injunction to support Native women *as Native women*, not just

Photo 13.2. A women's prayer walk to the blocked bridge on Highway 1806

as "women." It is in some ways similar to the hunter's claim in the car rental line that "this ain't no Indian land anymore . . . this is just America now," and reflects the preponderant invisibility of indigeneity as a specific identity.

On our return from this prayer walk, two white men stepped into the ranks of women and began chanting, "Mni Wiconi! Water is life!" While their intent may have been to show support, these men had been told very specifically that this was not a time for men's voices, but rather for indigenous women's voices to be heard. I later interviewed one of the Native women who had organized the walk and asked her about that moment. She sighed. "I don't know if that was patriarchy or racism. It was both. You see how our men stayed out of the way? Because they knew this was a time for us, not them, so they didn't make it about them. We have our own healing to do, but so do you white people. That wasn't right, what they did." I asked her why, then, no one had stopped the men from joining the ranks of women. She replied, "That's up to them to decide how to behave. We're not here to tell people what choices to make. Maybe that's how they were raised." She added, looking at me sharply, "We're not here for you. We're here for us."

This understanding of indigenous people as a collective ("us") separate from non-indigenous people ("you") was also expressed by the elder who complained of "white privilege" and the white woman who noted, "we're just visitors here." Equally important, though, was this leader's refusal to be responsible for the white men's behavior with her assertion that "we're not here to tell people what choices to make." The camps, the movement itself, and in fact most indigenous space I've encountered both at Standing Rock and elsewhere, have been marked by this same ethos of personal responsibility and refusal to strictly impose conformity to social expectations, reflecting a refusal to engage, on at least a micro level, with the actions of seeming allies but rather relying on a long-standing sense of collective identity.

At times this lack of strict enforcement seems to have been misinterpreted by non-Native visitors as either tacit approval of their actions or even as placing them and their actions outside of the community's norms. The white family and their camper, the white women and their singing, the white men and their chanting, and even the young white people dancing in the street through tendrils of marijuana smoke (in direct defiance of the "no drugs" policy) seemed to consider the rules and social mores of the community irrelevant and inapplicable to themselves or their actions. In some ways this reflects materialist feminists' Foucauldian claims that such frames are often constrained by outside structures; white supremacist ideologies, which have been described by sociologist Robin DiAngelo (2018) as not only pervasive but also almost irresistibly persuasive to white Americans, shape and inform the actions of even the most well-intentioned white allies.[3] And this in turn perhaps produces a dialectical response from Native people that indigeneity is "not that" as a response to white supremacist ideologies that enable such disregard for indigenous cultural practices.

DISCUSSION

Through the presence of the Lakota language, Lakota expectations of behavior, discourses about the gathering at Standing Rock as a ceremony, the deference shown to the leadership of elders, and the very structure of the camp as a place of welcome as long as expectations for behavior were met, the Lakota and their indigenous allies asserted their continued existence as distinct Peoples with a long, enduring presence. Indigenous people at Standing Rock exhibited and expressed a strong claim to indigenous identity that perhaps responded in some ways to non-Native claims, but was primarily rooted in long-standing existence and historical occupation as well as a sense of tradition-oriented behavior. The State and its actors, as well as everyday North Dakotans, resisted this narrative of enduring identity and instead described the Lakota and their Native allies as lawless protesters and even terrorists, if indigeneity was granted a valid existence at all. Perhaps somewhere in the middle of these competing claims lie the words and deeds of non-Native allies who themselves fail to recognize their own power and racial privilege such as the white women singing "Amazing Grace," and those like the white woman with whom I washed dishes, who recognized her status as a "guest" on someone else's land.

It is perhaps no surprise, then, that indigenous identity at Standing Rock was often expressed in opposition to other identities, particularly those racialized as white; "this is *our* land"; "you white people are new . . . but we've always been here"; "we're not here for you. We're here for us." At the same time, much of the framing around indigenous identity centered not an opposition to whiteness, but simply a long-standing existence, expressed through physical embodiment and cultural practice that can be traced back for centuries before "century" was a unit of time in what is now called the United States. In some ways, therefore, indigenous actors responded to the dominant culture's constraints and existing identity frames through their own assertions of indigenous identity; in other ways, however, their expressions of identity predate such structures and in fact reflected long-standing, though evolving, cultural practices.

The multiple framings of Standing Rock reflected a number of competing and colluding ideas about indigeneity in the twenty-first century: Native land on which others were guests, and where race was notable and implicated, brought together by the hospitality, at times strained, of Standing Rock Reservation; and an assertion of continued existence rooted in history and practice. These existed in tense opposition to the heavily militarized presence of local and state police, who, together with the National Guard, sought to surveil and contain *Oceti Sakowin* twenty-four hours a day, thus keeping the perceived and widely touted threat of angry Natives controlled and separated from the general (non-Native) population. Off the reservation, in the nearby city of Bismarck, non-Native understandings of what it means to be indigenous reflected a desire for unity that frequently subsumed indigeneity into a greater "American" identity, an ideological move that sought to delegitimize indigeneity as a valid, distinct identity.

For several months in 2016 and 2017, Standing Rock served as a visible center of competing and coalescing claims about indigenous identity and its multiple meanings and enactments, and offered a glimpse into the complexities of these at the beginning of the twenty-first century. Standing Rock illustrates the ongoing contest, begun just over five hundred years ago, to determine not only what indigeneity means but who has the power to define it. Native water protectors expressed their indigeneity in a myriad of ways, from their language and actions to their tradition-oriented behaviors. They explained both explicitly and implicitly that indigeneity has a long history on this continent, longer certainly than the history of non-Native presence, and that their continued existence does, in fact, render their identity somewhat unique. However, non-Native people often spoke louder, in the media and even in the camps, or simply didn't listen. This, too, frames indigeneity—not "hearing" Native women seeking to amplify their own voices, or not heeding the rules of the camp or the common courtesy of moving a vehicle, are ways of denying legitimacy to indigenous authority, even on indigenous land. They are ways of defining indigeneity as important or not, agential or not, distinct or simply subsumed into the broader culture.

I close with a brief story that I hope illustrates the difference between legitimacy granted or withheld by non-Native people over indigeneity's meaning, and legitimacy produced and maintained by Native people. On my last afternoon at Standing Rock I sat in the main circle of the camp watching indigenous visitors from Guatemala perform a dance in honor of the protectors. A boy I didn't know, perhaps ten years old, passed me a cup of coffee.

"*Lil-osní*, Auntie,"[4] he said shyly before ducking his head.

I managed a surprised "*Pilamaya!*" before he dashed away—but not before I caught a glimpse of his T-shirt, which had on it a picture of *Tatanka Iyotanka*, Sitting Bull, a revolutionary leader of the Lakota people, a man who himself alternately fought against and sought to live peacefully with the white people who had entered his land violently and illegally. The words underneath Tatanka Iyotanka's face read, "Not Your Indian."

No, *hoksila waste*,[5] I thought as I sipped my coffee and watched the dancers. You are not my Indian. You belong to the People, and the People are here.

NOTES

1. Many of those present at Standing Rock refute the months-long gathering as a "protest" against the pipeline, rather understanding it as defensive action intended to protect the Missouri River from oil contamination. However, as this chapter examines the multiple meanings of events at Standing Rock, I use both "protest" and "protect" throughout to acknowledge wider social and political framings of the presence of water defenders and their actions. Events at Standing Rock were both protection and protest, depending on who you are, why you went, and what you did there.

2. Following this conversation I also spoke to the woman in the camper, asking her to move their vehicle and pointing to the car that was driving through the grass in order to get around them. She told me she had to wait for her husband to get back. Maybe he never came back, because that camper never moved.

3. Including, I'm sure, my own.

4. "It's very cold" in Lakota; tradition-oriented Native people often refer to each other by relationship, and "auntie" is a kind of catch-all polite term for a woman too old to be a sister but too young to be a grandmother.

5. "Beautiful boy" in Lakota.

REFERENCES

Aroopala, Christy. 2012. "Mobilizing Collective Identity: Frames and Rational Individuals." *Political Behavior* 34(2): 193–224.

Barat, Frank. 2017. "Criminalizing Standing Rock." Al Jazeera, June 21. https://www.aljazeera.com/indepth/opinion/2017/06/criminalising-standing-rock-environmental-activism-170619090436488.html.

Berlinger, Sara. 2016. *Reporters Threatened at DAPL Protest Camp.* Posted October 19. https://www.kfyrtv.com/content/news/Reporters-threatened-at-DAPL-protest-camp-397668161.html.

Democracy Now. 2017a. "As Oil Starts to Flow Through Dakota Access Pipeline, Resistance Faces Paramilitary Security Force." *Democracy Now*, June 2. https://www.democracynow.org/2017/6/2/as_oil_starts_to_flow_through.

———. 2017b. "Private Security Firm TigerSwan Targets Pipeline Protesters in COINTELPRO-Like Operation." *Democracy Now*, June 2. https://www.democracynow.org/2017/6/2/part_2_private_security_firm_tigerswan.

DiAngelo, Robin. 2018. *White Fragility: Why It's So Hard for White People to Talk About Racism.* Boston: Beacon Press.

Hecht, Michael. 1993. "2002—A Research Odyssey: Toward the Development of a Communication Theory of Identity." *Communications Monographs* 60: 76–82.

Hennessy, Rosemary. 1993. *Materialist Feminism and the Politics of Discourse*. New York: Routledge.

McCleary, Mike. 2016a. "Decision on Easement Is Lousy Policy." *Bismarck Tribune*, December 11. https://bismarcktribune.com/news/opinion/editorial/decision-on -easement-is-lousypolicy/article_c52c0849-b0d6-5a1e-9038-5deb1d0a32fc.html.

———. 2016b. "Utilities Plan Could Benefit Tribe, State." *Bismarck Tribune*, December 23. https://bismarcktribune.com/news/opinion/editorial/utilities-plan -couldbenefit-tribe-state/article_a315bf69-9be8-5e20-a642-343b623c4bd6.html.

Naples, Nancy. 2002. "Materialist Feminist Discourse Analysis and Social Movement Research: Mapping the Changing Context for 'Community Control.'" In *Social Movements: Identity, Culture, and the State*, edited by David S. Meyer, Nancy Whittier, and Belinda Robnett, 226–46. New York: Oxford University Press.

———. 2003. *Feminism and Method: Ethnography, Discourse Analysis, and Activist Research*. New York: Routledge.

Ness, Ron. 2016. "Logic Should Prevail with DAPL." *Bismarck Tribune*, December 25. https://bismarcktribune.com/news/opinion/guest/logic-should-prevail-with -dapl/article_305fc527-d715-55dc-a2e7-2b76f9e82af1.html.

Silva, Daniella. 2016. "Dakota Access Pipeline: More Than 100 Arrested as Protestors Ousted from Camp." NBC News, October 28. https://www.nbcnews .com/storyline/dakota-pipeline-protests/dakota-access-pipeline-authorities-start -arresting-protesters-new-camp-n674066.

Sylvester, Terray. 2016. "North Dakota Officials Hope to Quell Pipeline Protests with Fines." Reuters, November 29. https://www.reuters.com/article/us-north-dakota -pipeline-idUSKBN13O2FD.

Tajfel, Henri. 2010. *Social Identity and Intergroup Relations*. Cambridge: Cambridge University Press.

Turner, J. C., and H. Tajfel. 1986. "The Social Identity Theory of Intergroup Behavior." In *Psychology of Intergroup Relations*, edited by S. Worchel and W. G. Austin, 7–24. Chicago: Nelson-Hall.

Chapter 14

This Is Hard

Researching and Writing Outside the Lines

Barbara Gurr

I began this project in spring 2016 when I first became aware of the small but growing movement on Standing Rock Reservation through personal and activist channels—that is to say, I entered this project through personal and political commitments, not academic ones. During my first trip to Standing Rock it became clear that this was a rich site from which to consider the complexities of indigenous identity, environmental justice, human rights, and the rule of law from multiple perspectives. My second trip to *Oceti Sakowin* camp, in November 2016, by which time the camp had swelled to over 7,000 occupants, provided an opportunity to consider more closely the role of indigenous leadership and tradition-oriented Lakota values as points of resistance as well as assertions of identity. By then, events at Standing Rock had captured broader attention, due largely to the work of Native activists on social media and the attention the mainstream media paid to the events of Sunday, November 20, when the police attacked water protectors on a barricaded bridge. But the people around me—students, colleagues, friends—were not hearing about these things, and what they did hear they didn't always have a context for.

Sociology has a unique critical lens to offer in such situations. As sociologists, our training allows us to think through social interactions in ways that can help clarify the role of history, or of political or social institutions, or of systemic racism. Sociology teaches us to ask questions that many other people don't ask. Feminist sociology reminds us to always keep power at the center of our questions. In this particular project, I'm asking who has the power. What does that power look like, sound like, act like? What does it produce, and what does it require? Just as importantly, who does *not* have power? Where is that almighty sociological concept, agency? In the chapter

I've written, I'm thinking through power (agency) to define oneself, both individually and collectively, particularly for Native people. But always, there are power dynamics in the research process, as well.

For example, when I first traveled to Standing Rock I brought supplies: water, propane, propane heaters, blankets, solar batteries. I didn't bring these things as a way to gain trust; I brought them because I was told they were needed. But did my offering of these things engender a sense of obligatory reciprocity on the part of the water defenders there? Perhaps, although had I not known the right way to behave at the camps, that wouldn't have lasted long. This brings to light the power that Native people and others exert in my research project. "Informants," as we call them in sociology, decide what to share, when to share, and even whether they will share. Additionally, as do many feminist researchers, I regularly "member check," which means I offer numerous opportunities to my informants to comment on the work at every stage, through in-person conversations, emails, phone calls, and even Facebook messaging. This is a way of sharing power over the construction of the story that emerges from the data, but must also be done carefully so as not to overburden my informants, all of whom, of course, live full and busy lives of their own and none of whom will directly benefit from this research (although it's always my hope that there will be a less tangible, collective benefit from sharing their stories; it is also important to note that a great deal of feminist sociological work is done specifically to produce change through community action or at the level of formal policy).

As a white scholar, I'm painfully aware that my racial privilege and the financial resources and social capital granted me by my advanced degrees often contribute to real and perceived race and class divides between myself and the Native people who may or may not welcome me into their communities, creating an uneasy insider-outsider dynamic as I navigate being both an occasional community member and also a researcher. My positionality as someone who has Native friends and relatives, relationships I have developed and treasured for twenty years, grants me a certain access, but my visible identity as a white woman together with my class status as a middle-class professor from Connecticut also set me apart from many Native people in important, material ways. All of these inform my presence in Native space. At some moments and in some spaces I'm fully welcome, but at others my presence is merely tolerated or may even be prohibited; it is of course incumbent upon me to recognize these differences and behave appropriately. Similarly, I often find myself included in spaces where I'm expected to understand more than I do, yet to ask for clarification would be rude or intrusive; here again, it's up to me to figure things out as best I can and seek clarification at a more appropriate time, or find ways to better understand that don't require the people around me to take the time to educate me or serve as a kind of "tour guide" to their lives.

Following data collection and member checking, primary control returns to me. I decide what to share more widely, how to share it, and even whether I will share it. For example, in the chapter I've written, I had to choose which stories to share and which to cut; whose voices would be heard and whose would not; what the central ideas that I, as a sociologist, determined should be shared in a chapter in a book on feminist research methods as opposed to, for example, an academic journal. The field of sociology also exerts influence here—as Dorothy Smith has noted, "a moment comes after talk has been inscribed as texts and becomes data when it must be worked up as sociology" (1999, 46). One example of this is my decision to refer to the people who shared their stories with me as "informants," rather than "relatives," which would centralize a more indigenous perspective of our relationship, but would take up precious word count to explain and justify. "Relatives" just doesn't sound as objective as "informants," does it? Sociology as a field continues to privilege certain forms of "objectivity" over others, despite the interventions of feminist scholars. The way I work through this project as a sociologist is different from the way a historian would, for example, and likely different from the way a Native water protector would. The final story I tell will reflect that.

There is also the practical consideration of how much to tell, after the data collection and analysis, when it's time to present or publish; I often find that non-Native people simply don't have enough knowledge of Native America for me to start in the middle, or even the beginning; frequently, much of my struggle with writing comes from how much background is needed, and how much will "fit" into publishing constraints. This became particularly clear to me when I transitioned my dissertation examining Native women's reproductive health care into a book and wrestled with the question of "how much is still not enough?" Perhaps this is unique to writing about Native America, but I suspect that all researchers, who are so often fascinated by our own areas of consideration, have a similar dilemma.

To address some of these concerns, when I write about Native America I try to do so from an auto-ethnographic perspective. As numerous scholars have pointed out (e.g., Denshire 2014; Diversi and Moreira 2009; Tomaselli, Dyll, and Francis 2008), auto-ethnography offers a potential transgression of sociological paradigms; frankly, it can be uncomfortable for both writer and reader. It's hard to continually note my presence, and it's unusual to continually see the researcher in an academic piece of writing, even an ethnography. That discomfort fascinates me, because it seems to signal how thoroughly "disciplined" we have become in sociology and academia generally. I also use auto-ethnography to remind us all that there are multiple ways of knowing, and it is perhaps to our disadvantage to over-privilege the ones with which we are most comfortable. Finally, auto-ethnography allows me to incorporate Sandra Harding's (1993) ideas about "strong objectivity," which is in its most basic form a kind of brutal honesty, a way of saying, "listen, I exist in this research as a full human being, and that means I come to it with a history and a belief system." I use auto-ethnography to be very clear about whose voice the reader is hearing and whose analysis is framing the story, but at the same time I am required, to some degree, to adopt a sociological perspective that potentially distances me from the analysis itself. That, too, is a kind of honesty; denying my role as an academic researcher would be just as disingenuous as denying my personal presence in the research.

Auto-ethnography has its pitfalls as well as its strengths. In my work, in which I seek to center the voices of Native people, I run the risk of doing the exact opposite by centering my own presence. The story seems to be about me, when I am in fact only the storyteller. I struggle with this (often, I'm sure, unsuccessfully). I insist on my transparent presence to avoid the potentially arrogant presumption of authority—"I'm nervous, I'm shy, I don't know everything"—but how do I do this and yet not stifle the voices of my informants when I only have seven thousand words or less? Striking the best balance often eludes me.

Most of my research to date has considered intersectional questions of gender, race, and sexuality. In my dissertation research, I examined Native women's reproductive health-care experiences, and although that work offered an intersectional analysis centering race, sexuality, and citizenship, it was primarily about gendered experiences. In this project, while gender and sexuality are salient, they occupy a somewhat muted place in both data collection and analysis as I give greater consideration to the intersections of race and identity. Does this seeming neglect of the essential dictum of feminist research—that it must concern gender and/or sexuality—make my current project less feminist? I don't think so. I think one can use feminist methods, feminist epistemologies, and feminist politics in any research area, and that in fact it is these that make a project "feminist" more than specific research questions. Some feminist scholars would likely disagree with me on this, preferring to center gender and/or sexuality as their analytic frame. That's actually great, because that disagreement keeps feminism and feminist work lively and interactive. If there were only one way to do this, we would grow stagnant. Comfortable. Feminist sociology should not make us comfortable. It should challenge us.

I believe that what makes this project feminist is the attention to power, including the ways in which I seek to recognize and share it with the participants in my research, for example, by meeting them where they are (the parking lot of a convenience store after work) rather than asking them to meet me at a different location, or by checking back with them to ensure that I've understood their language and intention correctly and giving them the opportunity to tell me more or ask for changes. My effort, no doubt clumsy at times, to analyze the data from an indigenous perspective that is not culturally mine but that *should*, of course, be centered in research about indigenous people may be further understood as feminist, or it may be understood as "decolonized" or by any of several other names (Mihesuah 2003; L. Smith 2002). Its central thrust, however, is sharing power over whose stories are told, how, and when. My attention to the role of women and gender, while not the driving force of my data collection or analysis in this project, also reflects my commitment to understanding power in all of its diffuse locations, particularly from an intersectional perspective. My reliance on auto-ethnography, an approach that insists on honesty and strong objectivity, ensures that my work is shaped and organized by a feminist effort to contextualize my data, and my presence, in transparent ways. Perhaps none of these are necessarily feminist in and of themselves, or necessary for research to be "feminist," but together I believe they organize my work in ways that are deeply feminist, regardless of the central analytic focus.

Feminist research is hard. Perhaps all research epistemologies are, in their own ways, although I think the integral attention to power-sharing that informs so much feminist work is an additional demand that many other approaches do not require, or at least not in the same ways. But feminist research is also exciting and interesting, important, and revelatory. I certainly hope my own work is also respectful and respectable. Feminist praxis demands that of me, and though I may sometimes fail to meet that demand, even in the failure there is learning and evolution and progress.

REFERENCES

Denshire, Sally. 2014. "On Auto-Ethnography." *Current Sociology* 62(6): 831–50.
Diversi, Marcelo, and Claudio Moreira. 2009. "Methodological Acts and Detours: A Dialogue on (Auto)ethnography." In *Betweener Talk: Decolonizing Knowledge Production, Pedagogy, and Praxis*, 183–204. Walnut Creek, CA: Left Coast Press.
Harding, Sandra. 1993. "Rethinking Standpoint Epistemology: What Is Strong Objectivity?" In *Feminist Epistemologies*, edited by Linda Alcoff and Elizabeth Potter, 49–82. New York: Routledge.
Mihesuah, Devon. 2003. *Indigenous American Women: Decolonization, Empowerment, Activism*. Lincoln: University of Nebraska Press.

Smith, Dorothy. 1999. *Writing the Social: Critique, Theory, and Investigations*. To-
ronto: University of Toronto Press.
Smith, Linda Tuhiwai. 2002. *Decolonizing Methodologies: Research and Indigenous
Peoples*. London: Zed Books.
Tomaselli, Keyan, Lauren Dyll, and Michael Francis. 2008. "'Self' and 'Other': Auto-
Reflexive and Indigenous Ethnography." In *Handbook of Critical and Indigenous
Methodologies*, edited by Norman K. Denzin, Yvonna S. Lincoln, and Linda Tuhi-
wai Smith, 347–73. Thousand Oaks, CA: Sage.

Appendix A

Key Elements of Research Design

The research design process begins with the initial plan for the project, often articulated in the form of a research proposal. While the initial research design often changes and evolves as the research is conducted, it is critical to begin with a plan for a systematic approach to data collection. The most important part of the research proposal is a solid research question. Some tips for crafting a good research question and examples of research questions are shown in box A.1.

When writing about research design in a final product (e.g., paper, article, book, thesis, dissertation), researchers articulate key information about how the project was carried out. This involves revising the methods section of the initial research proposal to reflect what actually occurred as well as adding detail about how the data was collected and analyzed. The elements of research design typically found in methods sections or chapters for the most common methods used by sociologists are detailed below. As you read the description of the methods in empirical research, you should be able to identify all the elements of the research design (and note any elements that may be missing). When you write up your own research, be sure to include all the relevant elements for your project!

INTERVIEWS AND FOCUS GROUPS

Data Collection

- Research method (e.g., qualitative interviews, semistructured interviews, in-depth interviews, focus groups)

- Criteria for participation (e.g., individual characteristics)
- Access and recruitment
- Sampling strategy (e.g., convenience, random)
- Number of interviews
- Year(s) interviews conducted
- Geographic location
- Type of space where interviews were conducted
- Average length (and/or range) of interviews
- State how interviews were audiotaped and transcribed

BOX A.1
Crafting a Good Research Question

Criteria for a good research question:

- Can be answered with the *method* being utilized
- Can be answered with the *data* being utilized
- Includes research design details necessary to make the research question answerable with the method and data (e.g., population, location, time frame)
- Is appropriate in scope for the proposed research design (i.e., not too broad, not too narrow)
- Does not make assumptions about what the findings will be

Example research questions from empirical chapters in this volume:

- How is shared parenting negotiated in lesbian, bisexual, and queer stepparent families formed after a relationship dissolution? (Acosta, chapter 3)
- Who are feminists in the United States today, and what do they believe about social inequality? (Harnois, chapter 5)
- How do parents raising children in poverty and social service providers working with poor families think about personal and social responsibility in relation to family, poverty, and public policy? (Kane, chapter 7)
- Drawing on the life story of Maxine Feldman, how does music become politicized when filtered through a lens of oppression, prejudice, and discrimination? (Reger, chapter 9)
- How do race and gender shape African American women's attitudes toward science? (Kelly et al., chapter 11)
- What assertions of indigeneity emerged and coalesced at Standing Rock? How were these events understood by different actors? How were those ways of understanding identity built, sustained, disseminated, and received? (Gurr, chapter 13)

- Any relevant identities of the researcher(s) and how these identities impact the research
- Demographics and other individual characteristics of participants relevant for the analysis (state that pseudonyms are used); use a demographics table if needed

Data Analysis

- Software (if used)
- Approach to data analysis (e.g., inductive, drawing on previous research or theory)
- Topics addressed in interviews and/or examples of questions
- Discussion of codes or themes

ETHNOGRAPHY AND PARTICIPANT OBSERVATION

Data Collection

- Research method (e.g., ethnography, participant observation)
- Description of the site or setting (use pseudonym for identifiable locations)
- Criteria and explanation for choosing the setting (specifically in relation to the research question)
- How the researcher entered the site (including gaining permission from gatekeepers if relevant)
- (Approximate) numbers and types of people in the site (note that names will be pseudonyms)
- Time in the setting (date range, number of visits, and/or number of hours)
- How the researcher took jottings/notes in the setting (if at all) and after leaving
- What kinds of data were collected (e.g., conversations, behavior)
- The degree to which the researcher was a participant in the setting
- Any relevant identities of the researcher(s) and how these identities impact the research

Data Analysis

- Software (if used)
- Approach to data analysis (e.g., inductive, drawing on previous research or theory)
- Discussion of codes or themes

QUALITATIVE OR QUANTITATIVE CONTENT ANALYSIS

Data Collection

- Research method (quantitative content analysis, qualitative content analysis, discourse analysis)
- Source of the data
- Criteria for inclusion in population: date range, key terms or topic, other criteria for inclusion
- Number of cases in population
- Number of cases in sample
- Sampling strategy (random, stratified, the population is the sample)
- Characteristics of the sample relevant for the analysis
- Any relevant identities of the researcher(s) and how these identities impact the research

Data Analysis

- Software (if used)
- Approach to data analysis (e.g., inductive, deductive, drawing on previous research or theory)
- Discussion of codes or themes

PRIMARY QUANTITATIVE DATA

Data Collection

- Research method (e.g., survey, experiment) and modality (e.g., telephone, face-to-face)
- Criteria for participation (e.g., individual characteristics)
- Access and recruitment
- Sampling strategy (e.g., convenience, random)
- Number of respondents
- Year(s) data gathered
- Geographic location
- Average length (and/or range) of surveys
- Any relevant identities of the researcher and how these identities impact data collection and analysis

Data Analysis

- Software
- Approach to data analysis (e.g., bivariate analysis, Ordinary Least Squares (OLS) regression)

- Measures (independent, dependent, control variables), including survey question wording (as relevant)
- Demographics and other individual characteristics of participants relevant for the analysis

SECONDARY QUANTITATIVE DATA

Data Collection

- Research method (e.g., secondary analysis of survey data)
- Source of the data and description of the dataset
- Any relevant identities of the researcher(s) and how these identities impact the research

Data Analysis

- Software
- Approach to data analysis (e.g., bivariate analysis, OLS regression)
- Measures (independent, dependent, control variables), including survey question wording (as relevant)
- Demographics and other individual characteristics relevant for the analysis

Appendix B

Further Resources

There is an extensive literature about feminist research in sociology and across disciplines. Below are some of the books and articles that have most influenced the contributors to this edited volume.

SCHOLARLY BOOKS AND ARTICLES ON FEMINIST RESEARCH

Bloom, Leslie Rebecca. 1998. *Under the Sign of Hope: Feminist Methodology and Narrative Interpretation.* Albany: State University of New York Press.

Cho, Sumi, Kimberlé Williams Crenshaw, and Leslie McCall. 2013. "Toward a Field of Intersectionality Studies: Theory, Applications, and Praxis." *Signs: Journal of Women in Culture and Society* 38(4): 785–810.

Clawson, Dan, Robert Zussman, Joya Misra, Naomi Gerstel, Randall Stokes, Douglas Anderton, and Michael Burawoy, eds. 2007. *Public Sociology.* Berkeley: University of California Press.

Compton, D'Lane, Tey Meadow, and Kristen Schilt, eds. 2018. *Other, Please Specify: Queer Methods in Sociology.* Oakland: University of California Press.

Connell, Raewyn. 2014. "Feminist Scholarship and the Public Realm in Postcolonial Australia." *Australian Feminist Studies* 29(80): 215–30.

DaCosta, Kimberly McClain. 2012. "The Tenure System, Disciplinary Boundaries, and Reflexivity." *Ethnic and Racial Studies* 35(4): 626–32.

Devault, Marjorie L. 1999. *Liberating Method: Feminism and Social Research.* Philadelphia: Temple University Press.

Emirbayer, Mustafa, and Matthew Desmond. 2011. "Race and Reflexivity." *Ethnic and Racial Studies* 35(4): 574–99.

Grauerholz, Liz, and Lori Baker-Sperry. 2007. "Feminist Research in the Public Domain: Risks and Recommendations." *Gender & Society* 21(2): 272–94.

Haraway, Donna. 1988. "Situated Knowledges: The Science Question in Feminism and the Privilege of Partial Perspective." *Feminist Studies* 14(3): 575–99.

Harding, Sandra. 1986. *The Science Question in Feminism.* Ithaca, NY: Cornell University Press.

———, ed. 1987. *Feminism and Methodology: Social Science Issues.* Bloomington: Indiana University Press.

———, ed. 2004. *The Feminist Standpoint Theory Reader: Intellectual and Political Controversies.* New York: Routledge.

Harnois, Catherine E. 2012. *Feminist Measures in Survey Research.* Thousand Oaks, CA: Sage.

———. 2017. *Analyzing Inequalities: An Introduction to Race, Class, Gender, and Sexuality Using the General Social Survey.* Thousand Oaks, CA: Sage.

Hesse-Biber, Sharlene Nagy, ed. 2014. *Feminist Research Practice: A Primer.* Thousand Oaks, CA: Sage.

Jaggar, Alison M. 1989. "Love & Knowledge: Emotion in Feminist Epistemology." In *Gender/Body/Knowledge: Feminist Reconstructions of Being and Knowing,* edited by A. M. Jaggar and S. R. Bordo, 145–71. New Brunswick, NJ: Rutgers University Press.

Katz-Fishman, Walda, and Jerome Scott. 2005. "Comments on Burawoy: A View from the Bottom." *Critical Sociology* 31: 372–74.

Kleinman, Sherryl, and Martha A. Copp. 1993. *Emotions and Fieldwork.* Newbury Park, CA: Sage.

McCall, Leslie. 2005. "The Complexity of Intersectionality." *Signs: Journal of Women in Culture and Society* 30: 1771–1800.

Mihesuah, Devon. 2003. *Indigenous American Women: Decolonization, Empowerment, Activism.* Lincoln: University of Nebraska Press.

Moore, Wendy Leo. 2011. "Reflexivity, Power, and Systemic Racism." *Ethnic and Racial Studies* 35(4): 614–19.

Naples, Nancy A. 2003. *Feminism and Method: Ethnography, Discourse Analysis, and Activist Research.* New York: Routledge.

Oakley, Ann. 2016. "Interviewing Women Again: Power, Time and the Gift." *Sociology: The Journal of the British Sociological Association* 50(1): 195.

Ramazanoglu, Caroline, and Janet Holland. 2002. *Feminist Methodology: Challenges and Choices.* Thousand Oaks, CA: Sage.

Reger, Jo. 2001. "Emotions, Objectivity and Voice: An Analysis of a 'Failed' Participant Observation." *Women's Studies International Forum* 24/25: 605–16.

Reinharz, Shulamit. 1992. *Feminist Methods in Social Research.* New York: Oxford University Press.

Risman, Barbara J. 2001. "Calling the Bluff of Value-Free Science." *American Sociological Review* 66(4): 605–11.

Smith, Dorothy E. 2005. *Institutional Ethnography: A Sociology for People.* Lanham, MD: AltaMira Press.

Smith, Linda Tuhiwai. 2002. *Decolonizing Methodologies: Research and Indigenous Peoples.* London: Zed Books.

Sprague, Joey. 2005. *Feminist Methodologies for Critical Researchers: Bridging Differences*. Walnut Creek, CA: AltaMira Press.

Sprague, Joey, and Heather Laube. 2009. "Institutional Barriers to Doing Public Sociology: Experiences of Feminists in the Academy." *American Sociologist* 40(4): 249–71.

St. Denny, Emily. 2014. "'The Personal Is Political Science': Epistemological and Methodological Issues in Feminist Social Science Research on Prostitution." *Journal of International Women's Studies* 16(1): 76–90.

Taylor, Verta, and Lelia Rupp. 2005. "When the Girls Are Men: Negotiating Gender and Sexual Dynamics in a Study of Drag Queens." *Signs: Journal of Women in Culture and Society* 30(4): 2115–39.

RESEARCH METHODS CASES

The SAGE Research methods cases publish short pieces in which researchers reflect on the research process (http://methods.sagepub.com/cases). Below are a few that focus on feminist research.

Guntram, Lisa, and Ericka Johnson. 2018. "Feminist Approaches to Using Other People's Words: Two Examples." *SAGE Research Methods Cases.*

Holdsworth, Ella. 2015. "Feminist Approaches to Interviewing: Women's Experiences of Electronic Monitoring." *SAGE Research Methods Cases.*

Moronez, Jessica C. 2014. "Feminist Approaches to In-Depth Interviewing and Ethnographic Fieldwork: A Study of Male Anti-Violence Advocacy Groups." *SAGE Research Methods Cases.*

O'Keeffe, Suzanne. 2017. "The Interview as Method: Doing Feminist Research." *SAGE Research Methods Cases.*

Stock, Inka. 2018. "Ethnography, Reflexivity and Feminism: Researching Sub-Saharan African Migrants' Perspective on (Im)mobility in Morocco." *SAGE Research Methods Cases.*

MONOGRAPHS BY FEMINIST RESEARCHERS

Many monographs by feminist researchers have a chapter or appendix in which the authors reflect on the research process. Below are some of the contributors' favorite recent feminist monographs.

Acosta, Katie L. 2013. *Amigas y Amantes: Sexually Nonconforming Latinas Negotiate Family*. New York: Rutgers University Press.

Best, Amy. 2000. *Prom Night: Youth, Schools and Popular Culture*. New York: Routledge.

Bobel, Chris. 2010. *New Blood: Third-Wave Feminism and the Politics of Menstruation*. New Brunswick, NJ: Rutgers University Press.

Crossley, Alison D. 2017. *Finding Feminism: Millennial Activists and the Unfinished Gender Revolution*. New York: New York University Press.

Davis, Georgiann. 2015. *Contesting Intersex: The Dubious Diagnosis*. New York: New York University Press.

Gurr, Barbara. 2015. *Reproductive Justice: The Politics of Health Care for Native American Women*. New Brunswick, NJ: Rutgers University Press.

Harris, Deborah A., and Patti Giuffre. 2015. *Taking the Heat: Women Chefs and Gender Inequality in the Professional Kitchen*. New Brunswick, NJ: Rutgers University Press.

Kane, Emily W. 2012. *The Gender Trap: Parents and the Pitfalls of Raising Boys and Girls*. New York: New York University Press.

Kolb, Kenneth H. 2014. *Moral Wages: The Emotional Dilemmas of Victim Advocacy and Counseling*. Oakland: University of California Press.

Mazelis, Joan Maya. 2017. *Surviving Poverty: Creating Sustainable Ties among the Poor*. New York: New York University Press.

Moore, Mignon. 2011. *Invisible Families: Gay Identities, Relationships, and Motherhood among Black Women*. Berkeley: University of California Press.

Pfeffer, Carla. 2017. *Queering Families: The Postmodern Partnerships of Cisgender Women and Transgender Men*. New York: Oxford University Press.

Reger, Jo. 2012. *Everywhere and Nowhere: Contemporary Feminism in the United States*. New York: Oxford University Press.

Weitz, Rose. 2004. *Rapunzel's Daughters: What Women's Hair Tells Us About Women's Lives*. New York: Farrar, Straus and Giroux.

Wingfield, Adia Harvey. 2012. *No More Invisible Man: Race and Gender in Men's Work*. Philadelphia: Temple University Press.

VIDEO AND PODCASTS

We have identified some videos and podcasts about feminist research. These are from the podcasts "Give Methods a Chance" (https://thesocietypages.org/methods/) and Sage (http://methods.sagepub.com/). New segments are posted to both regularly. Below are some recent selections featuring feminist research.

Green, Kyle. 2015. "Amy Schalet on In-Depth Interviews." *Give Methods a Chance* (podcast).

———. 2016. "C. J. Pascoe on Ethnographic Research." *Give Methods a Chance* (podcast).

Henry, Marsha. 2015. "What Is Feminist Qualitative Research?" *Sage* (video). http://methods.sagepub.com.

Hesse-Biber, Sharlene. 2015. "What Is Feminist Empiricist Research?" *Sage* (video). http://methods.sagepub.com.

————. 2017. "Sharlene Hesse-Biber Discusses Feminist Research and Mixed Methods." *Sage* (video). http://methods.sagepub.com/video/sharlene-hesse-biber -discusses-feminist-research-and-mixed-methods.

WEBSITES

The following websites cover a variety of topics related to feminist research. There are regularly new posts on these sites.

The Society Pages: https://thesocietypages.org/feminist
Gender & Society Blog: https://gendersociety.wordpress.com

Index

Acosta, Katie, 5, 117

action research (AR), 18n1

adoption: agencies, same-sex couples denials by, 35; second-parent, 21, 22

Affordable Care Act, on home visiting programs, 66

African American women, 4; attitudes toward science, 101–15, *109*, *110*, 117–21; health-care system mistrust by, 102; science exclusion of, 7, 15; trust in science by, 102. *See also* science, African American women attitudes toward

age: feminist identity and, 57–58; feminists, on social inequality and, 43, *45*, *46*, *48*, *50*

agency, as a sociological concept, 61, 68, 73–75, 124, 141–42

AIM. *See* American Indian Movement

Allen, K. R., 22

American Indian Movement (AIM), 131, 132, 134

American National Election Survey (ANES), 2016, 39; data collection after 2016 presidential election, 42; on feminist identity, 40; Survey Documentation and Analysis program access to, 59

analytic strategy, in research, 107

Anderson, Jamie, 94

ANES. *See* American National Election Survey

"Angry Atthis" song, of Feldman, 83–84, 86–87, 91, 93; emotions related to, 98–99

AR. *See* action research

archival research, 13; emotions use in, 97–98; Feldman and, 97–100; feminism in, 97–100; at Standing Rock, 125

assisted reproduction technologies: lesbian couples and, 21; sperm donor selection in, 27–28

Atlas.ti qualitative coding software program, 17

auto-ethnography: qualitative methods of, 13–14, 126, 143–45; writing perspective, on Native Americans, 143, 145

Avenue of Flags, at *Oceti Sakowin*, 131, 132

Baca Zinn, Maxine: on multiracial feminism, 55; on relationality, 55–56

Biblarz, T. J., 36

159

About the Contributors

Maura Kelly is an associate professor of sociology at Portland State University. Her research and teaching interests include gender, sexualities, social inequality, work and occupations, and popular culture. Her current research is primarily focused on the experiences of women and people of color in the construction trades as well as policy and programs intended to increase the diversity of the construction trades workforce.

Barbara Gurr is an associate professor in residence with the Women's, Gender and Sexuality Studies Program at the University of Connecticut. She is the author of *Reproductive Justice: The Politics of Health Care for Native American Women* and the editor of *Race, Gender and Sexuality in Post-Apocalyptic TV and Film*. Currently she is working on two scholarly projects: an interdisciplinary, multiauthored examination of feminism in *Mad Max: Fury Road*, and an examination of environmental justice and human and cultural rights emerging from recent events at Standing Rock Reservation in North Dakota.

Katie Acosta is an associate professor in the department of sociology at Georgia State University. Her research and scholarly interests center on the intersections of gender, sexuality, Latinx studies, race/ethnicity, family, and immigration. She is the author of *Amigas y Amantes: Sexually Nonconforming Latinas Negotiate Family*, which explores the ways in which sexually nonconforming Latinas manage relationships with their partners, families of origin, and families of choice. She is working on her second book, *Stepping into Queer Parenting*, which centers on the social, legal, and interpersonal experiences of LBQ stepparent families. She is also writing on the potential for the advancement of "queerer" family scholarship using Anzaldúan theory.

Gordon Gauchat is an assistant professor of sociology at the University of Wisconsin–Milwaukee. His research focuses on the interaction of public perceptions of science and political and cultural cleavages in the United States and Europe. He has published research in *American Sociological Review*, *Social Forces*, *Nature Climate Change, Climatic Change, Gender and Society*, and *Public Understanding of Science*. His interests also include political-cultural identities, including left-right ideological orientations in the United States. He is currently studying public perceptions of scientists in various contexts as well as studying general attitudes toward science.

Catherine Harnois is a professor of sociology at Wake Forest University. Her research and teaching interests include social inequality, research methods, social psychology, gender, and intersectionality. Her research brings an intersectional theoretical perspective and quantitative methodological framework to the study of identity, political consciousness, and discrimination. She is the author of two books on social science research methods: *Feminist Measures in Survey Research* and *Analyzing Inequalities: An Introduction to Race, Class, Gender & Sexuality Using the US General Social Survey*.

Emily W. Kane is a professor of sociology, and a member of the Program in Gender and Sexuality Studies, at Bates College in Lewiston, Maine. She is the author of *The Gender Trap: Parents and the Pitfalls of Raising Boys and Girls* and *Rethinking Gender and Sexuality in Childhood* as well as articles and book chapters on a variety of topics. Her teaching, research, and public engagement focus on inequalities of race, class, gender, and sexuality, with particular attention to family and childhood.

Joyce McNair is a master's candidate in the sociology department at Portland State University. Her research focuses on exiting homelessness, framing of the homeless, and social stigma of the homeless.

Jo Reger is a professor of sociology at Oakland University in Michigan. Her books include *Everywhere and Nowhere: Contemporary Feminism in the United States, Different Wavelengths: Studies of The Contemporary Women's Movement* (editor), *The Oxford Handbook of Women's Social Movement Activism* (coeditor), and *Identity Work in Social Movements* (coeditor). Her latest research project examines music and the women's movement of the 1960s–1980s.

Elizabeth Withers is a doctoral candidate in the sociology department at Portland State University. Her research interests include racial and class-based health disparities. She is currently working on her dissertation, "Access in the Digital Field and Health Outcomes," which examines the effects of digital access on health outcomes.